THE HOLLOW MASK

A story of One Man's Redemption

Scott Ash

© 2023 Scott Ash

THE HOLLOW MASK
A story of One Man's Redemption

All rights reserved. No portion of this book may be reproduced, stored in a retrieval system, or transmitted in any form or by any means—electronic, mechanical, photocopy, recording, scanning, or other—except for brief quotations in critical reviews or articles, without the prior written permission of the publisher.

ISBN 978-1-73243-7197

info@guardianangelpress.com

Dedication

My life ... written page by page, chapter by chapter.... Trials and tribulations, utter rejection, unwanted and unloved, along with so many great failures. Written boldly, confidently, at times most ruthlessly.... Full of disappointment, desperation, and hopelessness.

But when You, Lord Jesus Christ, took my hand into Your hand, a new page and chapter begun.... Starting light and easy, with a slight degree of elegance.... And slowly, my handwriting began to bear Your handwriting, with increasingly bold strokes capturing Your unconditional love, kindness, forgiveness, grace, and unmerited mercy, which are now flowing across the pages of this book. You were there every step of the way!

To You, Lord Jesus Christ and Your Promise. To "Das Diva", for demonstrating Your unconditional love and being there every step of the way while writing this. I love you very much. And to "Sis C.," you were right, thank you! And the most special of thanks to Brother Igor. Proverbs 27:17 says, "Iron sharpens iron, and one man sharpens another." HE brought you into my life just at the right moment; thanks for sharpening me.

"See, I will not forget you for I have carved Your name on the palms of My hands". (Isaiah 49:16)—Thank you, Chief (****)

Who Am I

Well, my name is Chase.... I will be turning sixty this year. I cannot begin to count the times I have asked this gut-wrenching question, especially since I basically did not have loving or caring parents. I did not know them very much at all—very distant, lots of verbal and emotional attacks, physical punishment included, which could be overly explosive on so many occasions (leaving not just horrible physical wounds, but over time, deep psychological and emotional ones as well). This, I remember, happened almost every day.

I remember that our family lived in a barn for a good while with just mattresses on the floor. We ate from a table and sat on benches completely made of cement—it was cold. It struck me many years later as being cold like my parents. I don't really care sitting on cement benches to this day.

Our family did not enjoy a good reputation in our small town. I remember this very well. I had the feeling they viewed us as an outcast family, basically people to avoid, with others crossing over to the other side of the street, looking on in disgust. When two or more were together, one could clearly hear them chuckling and scoffing and pointing fingers….

It was hard. We were poor.

My father would come home drunk on Friday evenings, often tripping on the front door steps and injuring himself. I remember seeing his blood…. He would barely make it to his bed, where he would pass out in a drunken stupor, sometimes naked, with his soiled clothing strewn about on the floor….

It seemed that I was the one always chosen to clean up the blood; I loathed doing it.

I remember my mother verbally pummeling each of us to "get his paycheck" (he got paid in cash every Friday after work), and that meant either confronting him about the money or going into his room to go through his clothes to find it…. When she was not successful pushing me to do that, she would utter, "Go to hell!" or "I hate you!"

Oh, how I learned very quickly to deeply despise Friday evenings. I remember trying to "just not be there." I was a very small-built boy, effeminate, constantly being teased by my peers. I was experiencing great emotional, verbal, and, yes, a lot of physical abuse—so I knew so well being especially hated and scorned by that small town. That made going to sporting events or dances, etc., at my school out of the question. I just tried to disappear to a place where I could be alone, shouting at times at the very top of my voice, to someone I did not know at that time, "Who Am I?"

There was so much anger at home. I disliked my father and my mother. I found myself wishing them ill will. I had no earthly idea about what it meant to love and honor my parents as God's Word teaches us in Exodus 20:12. I remember the second part of that verse taunting me with "that Your days may be long in the land that the Lord God is giving you." I thought back then that because I was not honoring my parents, I will have a short life.

We attended a small, conservative church in our town. My memories there are of Reverend Moore, who would preach on God's unconditional love, His forgiveness, His mercy, His grace—following up each sermon with a call to the altar to "confess, repent, and give Your life to Jesus Christ," and to "be born again." If not, fire and brimstone would be hurled down and one would be tortured and burned in the eternal pit of hell (I can still see the Reverend's waving fists and his pounding on the pulpit, several times mentioning the "reprobate and depraved sodomites, adulterers, fornicators, the immoral," etc.). That scared me so much.

But even with that, I remember that the last thing I wanted to do was to be "born again." Once was enough for me, with all that I had badly experienced.

One thing about me was I was an excellent and overachieving student. I poured myself into my studies. It was not just an escape. I thought that maybe I could use it to please my parents. Perhaps, bringing home good grades would make them accept me and recognize my achievements and praise me with, "Hey, that's a good job, Son," and that my mother might think twice about using that broom and let me escape yet another punishment for things I did not do.

It didn't happen that way. The violence continued and would get worse. In fact, I do not much recall either of my parents calling me "son." It was more like "son of a bitch." In his later years, my father would write to me, finally addressing me as "son"—too little, too late in my opinion at the time.

So, back to Reverend Moore and his constant babbling of, "You must be born again." As an early academic, I knew I could not be physically born again, just as the Pharisee Nicodemus, a member of the ruling Jewish Council, said to Jesus in John 3:4, "How can a man be born when he is old? Surely, he cannot enter a second time into the mother's womb to be born again!"

Stopping at that verse, I did not really know what that meant—not so much in the spiritual sense, but from the standpoint that, at that time and from a very early age, all I wanted was to die and be done with my miserable life; to escape the violence, the hate, the constant rejection, the continual heaping on of guilt and shame from my parents.

I often remember thinking, *What did I do wrong? Why can I not please them? Why do they hate me so much? Why do I get physically punished so much?*

So, the last thing I wanted to listen to was "to be born again." I think it was around this time that I started to develop an outright dislike of God, whom I blamed for what I had been through—the idea of "repenting, confessing, and giving my life to Jesus" was the farthest thing from my mind at that time.

More to follow about this, but let's go back to the question that I asked at the beginning, "Who Am I?" and specifically as it relates to my position or standing with God if I would have believed in Him.

First, let's talk about knowing God. I remember listening to some sermons explaining that our worth and value in God is not based on us regarding who we are or anything that we have or could do, but solely on what God did for us, specifically sending His Son to die for us to reestablish a broken relationship that existed between God and mankind.

Second, in accepting Jesus as our Lord and Savior, we are saved and have a new identity in Him, with our new citizenship being sealed in His Kingdom.

So I said, "OK, this seems to make sense to me. I would have a new identity, but please reveal to me who I am in You when that happens." Let's take a look at some Bible verses that answer this very question.

2 Corinthians 5:17

"Therefore, if anyone is in Christ, he is a new creation. The old has passed away; behold, the new has come."

Ephesians 2:10

"For we are His workmanship, created in Christ Jesus for good works, which God prepared beforehand, that we should walk in them."

1 Peter 2:9

"But you are a chosen race, a royal priesthood, a holy nation, a people for his own possession, that you may proclaim the Excellencies of him who called you out of darkness into his marvelous light.

John 1:12

"But to all who did receive Him, who believed in His name, He gave the right to become children of God."

2 Corinthians 5:21

"For our sake he made him to be sin who knew no sin, so that in him we might become the righteousness of God."

Ephesians 2:6

"And raised us up with HIM and seated us with HIM in the heavenly places in Christ Jesus."

John 15:15

"No longer do I call you servants, for the servant does not know what his master is doing; but I have called you friends...."

Galatians 3:26

"For in Christ Jesus you are all sons of God, through faith."

Romans 8:17

"And if *children—heirs of God and fellow heirs with Christ*, provided we suffer with him in order that we may also be glorified with him.

1 John 4:4

"Little children, you are from God.…"

Philippians 3:20

"But our citizenship is in heaven.…"

1 Corinthians 12:27

"Now you are the Body of Christ and individually members of it.

1 Corinthians 6:17

"But he who is joined to the Lord becomes one spirit with Him"

Romans 5:1

"Therefore, since we have been justified by faith, we have peace with God.…"

John 15:16

"You did not choose me, but I chose you.…"

And there or so many more verses talking about who we are in Christ.

After looking up the verses, I discovered that I had so many questions:

A new creation?

His workmanship?

A chosen race?

A royal priesthood?

A holy nation?

A people for His own possession?

Children of God?

The righteousness of God?

Seated with Him in the heavenly places?

Friends?

Sons of God?

Heirs of God?

Fellow Heirs with CHRIST?

From GOD?

Citizenship in Heaven?

The Body of Christ?

Individual members of that Body?

Joined to the Lord?

One Spirit with Him?

Justified?

Peace with God?

Chosen?

Hmm, that's a lot of what the Word of God says that I am in Christ Jesus and with God. A lot to mull over for a very young boy who was scorned, rejected, abandoned, abused, unwanted, unloved, shamed, guilted, totally imperfect, and extremely marginalized.

And in Sunday School, being the inquisitive one, I would often find myself in the position of wanting to find out more, but we got told the answers before we could even ask the questions. I heard on several occasions that it is what it is, which meant to me to not even ask questions but just accept the answer. It was a very conservative church, where speaking in Sunday School, or in Church, was not welcomed.

And now, almost fifty years later, I find my thoughts returning to Reverend Moore, who is most likely now dancing with Jesus. So, what he was always going on about this Jesus—whom I had come to so dislike—offering me to be saved, born again, and about who we are in Christ; all so absolutely foreign to me: could he have possibly been making sense? I wish now that things would have been different—much different.

When I was ten years old, a patrol car showed up at our house. The policeman knocked on the door and, once in, said they had an arrest warrant for me.

Instinctively, I asked why.

The policeman said I was under arrest and would take me with him.

I looked longingly at my parents for help, but they would not even look at me; they did not even get up from the couch. In that very moment, I felt pure and utter rejection. The policeman took me by the arm to the police car. I looked back towards the house (the door had been closed), desperately hoping that my parents would at least do something. They did not.

Once in the police car, the policeman told me to just sit and be quiet. I was sobbing uncontrollably, not knowing what was happening or what would come. I just stared out the back window, hoping to see my parents' car behind us, but I did not. I was very lonely and once again feeling unwanted and unworthy.

We arrived at the county jail and I remember getting processed in and asking about what was happening and where my parents were.

I was once again told to just sit and be quiet. After what seemed like an eternity, a policeman came and told me that I would be staying there at the jail until they could "figure out" what to do with me. He led be by my arm down what seemed like a long and dark hallway and took me into a jail cell with a barred door. He told me that I would get dinner and then I go to bed. I tried to ask where my parents were and what was going on but received no answer. I was devastated and never felt more alone than at that point.

So there I was, in a jail cell at ten—and what were the benches and tables made of? Cement.

That alone brought many painful memories of living in a barn; they looked exactly the same as then.

I ate standing up and then was told to go to bed in the clothing I was wearing. I did that and lay down, with so many thoughts and questions running through my head—where are my parents, why is this happening, what did I do this time that led to an arrest? I was so confused, and my thoughts were racing everywhere. I cried uncontrollably. Even then, I knew that getting arrested was not a good thing, and I was anxious where things would go from there.

At some point, I fell asleep. During the night, I was jarred awake and realized that I was being raped by a male who turned out to be in a separate cell in the larger cell room. The entire cell had three individual cells and those doors were open. I did not realize that when they placed me in my cell. It was a horrible nightmare. I was terrified and just wanted to die even at that very young age.

It turned out that the male who raped me was a classmate of my older sister. His name was Chuck. I knew a bit about him from seeing him at school or when he spent time with my sister. He did unthinkable and despicable things to me. I felt like an object for his personal gratification. I was terrified, and the pain was so extreme. He pressed his right-hand palm tightly against my mouth so that I could not scream. With his other hand, he held my two arms tightly together behind my back so that I could not move. He also told me to keep my mouth shut and not say anything to the police or it would just get worse for me.

After the attack, he picked up and threw me on the bed, mumbled something, and left. It was like a huge nightmare. And yet again, where was help? My parents, the jail guards, God, anyone? None came. The abuse went on for several days.

The police would not believe me, and I knew from experience that my parents would not believe me. If that was the case, who was going to believe me? So, I kept quiet on the outside while raging on the inside. The pain Chuck inflicted upon me, both physically and emotionally, were devastating and left deep wounds that would terribly scar me for life.

One morning, a policeman came with a juvenile hall worker. I was told I would be transferred to a juvenile hall and await what would happen to me. Again, no parents. I asked several times about them and received no answer.

So, I was released from the jail and taken to the juvenile hall. I was with a case worker. Many children, younger and older, were there. I was terrified that another assault would occur.

I was at that place for a good while. The abuse continued there, and still I was too afraid to say anything. It came to a point where I questioned myself: What was worse for me, the sexual, emotional, or physical abuse? A hard question for a ten-year-old boy to answer. I just wanted to die and considered ending my life right then and there. I must admit that I sometimes look back and wish I had done it.

One day, the case worker told me they had arranged for a court hearing. I asked what this was about and the case worker did not answer other than to tell me to be still and quiet. Our destination was the courthouse. I was led in by the case worker and met briefly with a lawyer, an individual who clearly had no interest in being there.

We sat down at the table and I realized my parents came in shortly after. I tried to get their attention to no avail. It was heartbreaking. The hearing started with the judge briefly stating that the purpose of the hearing was to make me a ward of the state. I did not know what that meant, so I asked the lawyer, who told me this means my parents would no longer have legal custody or responsibility for me. I recall thinking, *What is happening?*

Before I could think any further, the judge said —and those were the only words he said—I was in effect a ward of the state and that a solution would have to be found for me.

Over my left shoulder, I looked briefly at my parents. They would not look at me; their heads were turned downwards.

It was all a huge blur, so confusing, and I was going through so much turmoil. As the bailiff led me away, I looked again in the direction of my parents, who had gotten up and left the courtroom without even acknowledging me in any way.

I was taken back to the juvenile hall and told I would stay there until something happened. To this date, I have never been able to find out exactly what charges were made against me and why it all happened. And several years later when I did ask my mother, I did not get an answer. It haunted me tremendously.

I was in the juvenile hall for several weeks, existing in a daze and very confused. I was on medicines that seemed to make me worse—to quiet me down is what I had been told. So, with that, I pretended to swallow them, but after the staff who gave them to me turned around, I would spit them out. I hated it there. It was horrible.

One day, the case worker said they had found a potential foster home for me. I asked, "Why a foster home? Why could I not go back home to my parents?"

The response: "Because that is the way it is." – just like in Sunday School.

The next day, an older couple came to the home and were introduced to me. I was told in advance that they could not have children and wanted to foster one. The case worker told me that the foster home was located on a big ranch; that did excite me, along with them telling me I would be an only child. My first thought was that, maybe finally, I have found people who would take care of me and love me unconditionally.

At first glance, Robert and Carolyn seemed nice enough. I quickly noted that Carolyn was very affectionate to me right away, happy to potentially find a foster child.

When she attempted to take me in her arms and hug me, I flinched and stepped back, thinking there might be punishment involved with a broom or some other blunt object, triggered by what happened so many times before.

She did manage to get me into her arms, and it was not as horrible as I thought. I remember her almost whispering to the case worker that it looked as though I had been through a lot, and that this would require, in her words which I will never forget, "a whole hell of lot of work."

Right then, I asked myself a question: "Have I already become a burden to these people as well?"

Robert, on the other hand, was very distant. He did not say much except that I was too scrawny and needed some meat on my bones. He added that the ranch would do me good and if he had to, he would beat some manhood into me. I found out later what exactly he meant by those words.

Finally, a decision was made that I would become a foster child to Robert and Carolyn.

Before being released from the juvenile hall, I was allowed to go back to my parents' house. I really did not want to go back there; it was a place of pure hate and rejection for me.

When the case worker drove me there and knocked on the door, my mother answered it. She led us in and, in that moment, I found out very quickly that she knew I was coming to pick up my belongings. What little I had she placed in a few boxes just inside the doorway. I remember crying and just could not bring myself to say anything. I was so afraid.

As I was leaving with the case worker, a former classmate approached me. Without knowing what happened to me in jail, he told me that a schoolmate boy, named Chuck had died, adding that his wrecked vehicle was in the car junk lot just behind my parents' house across the railway tracks. While drunk, he drove full frontal into a train, killing him instantly.

The case worker and I left my parents' house with just a curt goodbye. As we were about to pass the junk lot, I asked the case worker if we could stop for a moment. For some reason, he said yes.

The lot's front gate was almost always closed, and the place was secured with high walls, but on that day, the gate was open. The case worker allowed me to go into the open lot.

I noted that there were no workers present. Then, there almost directly before me was a car totally wrecked and shattered. I approached the car, instinctively knowing that it did belong to my jail rapist. Standing on the driver's side, I stuck my head into the vehicle.

The compartment was full of his blood, splattered everywhere. Oddly enough, my next thought was, *what were his last thoughts? What was going through his highly inebriated mind and body?* But I did ask myself a question—*Why should he be allowed to check out of life so early, and why am I still here?*

I really did not have bad thoughts about him then. By nature, I have generally been a forgiving person (or so I thought). At that moment, my heart was very heavy. I was very sad and sorry for him. I took a step back from that car, collapsed to my knees and began to cry uncontrollably. Even as a ten-year-old child, I knew in that moment that this was an individual who would change the course of my life in so many ways, and forgiving him for what he had so violently put me through in that jailhouse.

After returning to the juvenile hall, I was a bit excited and somewhat hopeful that maybe I had found a home and parents. But what Robert and Carolyn said at our first meeting left me extremely apprehensive. A part of me was wary that I might be getting into more abuse and rejection rather than love.

Finally, the day came for the case worker to transfer me to the foster home. So I again packed the few belongings I had. On the drive there, he told me I should make the most of this special opportunity and not to mess up like before; that if I did not, worse things would become of me.

He said something that has stayed with me since: that punks like me needlessly burden the system, that it would be better if I were not there. The tone of his voice and his message led me to once again entertain the idea of taking my life.

How clearly the "go to hell" statements I had heard so many times came back to me. Again, my thought was that I was never really wanted or loved. It struck me even young age that hell seemed to be the place predestined for me. Maybe they were right: hell was where I would ultimately wind up.

We drove to the ranch in complete silence. When we arrived, the case worker turned to me and his final words to me were that he already knew that I would mess things up here as well and that I would most likely wind up in "the hall" again, with even worse consequences. That was not a very reassuring thing to hear, and in that moment, as I was getting out of the car, and seeing Robert and Carolyn standing there, and Robert making the comment that he was going to fix or break me, my mind was already preparing for even more abuse and rejection. It was very frightening.

The ranch was very large, along with the main house, where I had a shimmer of hope that I had finally had everything, to include my own room, where I was told by Robert that I should be lucky just to be there and that I should not mess things up like I did with my parents, but if I did, it was eerily similar to the comments that the case worker made to me. And so I set out to prove them all wrong, and if in doing so, I would in return please and satisfy them, and then hopefully I would be accepted and loved.

Things started off fairly well there. I was given a very large room with my own bathroom. It was located at the far end of the house, completely on the other side from where Robert and Carolyn's bedroom was, so I initially felt good to have the physical distance between us. I unpacked what little I had and there were some clothes, shoes, and other items that they had purchased for me. After unpacking, I got into the shower and it had to have been the longest and hottest shower I have ever taken, just standing there using a washcloth and soap in an attempt to wash off all the filth that had taken place. And also, the shame and guilt that I had with blaming everything on me personally. I scrubbed and scrubbed, so much so that my skin became wounded and was bleeding in several places. Seeing my own blood, I thought of Chuck's blood, no longer flowing through his body. I managed to stop the bleeding and got dressed.

At dinner, Robert told me how meals would work. I was to sit down and keep quiet and not speak unless spoken to. There was very light conversation with Carolyn asking me if I got unpacked and settled in a bit. The food was very delicious, considering what had been served in the jail and the juvenile hall. That was a comfort to me.

After we finished dinner, I was instructed that I would clean the table, take the dishes to the kitchen and wash them. I liked milk with my meals, and still do, and Robert and Carolyn had milk cows, so we had fresh milk. After I had washed and dried the dishes, Carolyn taught me how to clean the fresh milk bottles with very hot water and pure vinegar in order to clean them thoroughly and sanitize them. The water was so hot that I could hardly hold the bottles while trying to clean them. Robert noticed my intense struggling and commented that the process would help me become a real man. And then he said that this would most likely not work, and I had not proven any worth up until then, so why should things change now. That devastated me.

I would like to note here that while Robert said he would make me into a man, Carolyn, on the other side, told me early on that her real desire was to have a girl, but after Robert was so adamant in the selection of a male foster child, she reluctantly gave in, but never failed to mention this to me many, many times. She would tell me how she would raise a girl, how that girl would become proper and ladylike. She would go into detail on how she would dress the girl with beautiful clothing, pig tails, and shiny shoes. She said that would have pleased her the most.

Those words "please her most," instilled in me the thought that if were a girl, she would love and care for me more. I wanted to please her, and it confused me then and made me in a way ashamed to be a boy, with the feeling of being born into a wrong body. Wow, questioning Your own gender at such a young age, and after what all happened to me, I knew that I would most likely fail to please Robert in becoming a man, and failing to please Carolyn that I was not a girl, even at one point even telling me that she was disappointed that I was a boy. That hurt so bad and I was so confused. So I started to hate the body I was born into.

My already so confused mind was made even more confused as to why I was born a boy. And all of this at the tender age of eleven.

I was told after cleaning everything up that I would be starting school the next day, no time to waste. I hardly slept that night while in complete terror as to what bad would happen next. That's how my young mind was programmed by then, to always look for bad and terrible things to suddenly come upon me. Morning came far too quickly. As I came into the kitchen, I was greeted with Robert's comment that he expected me not to mess this up or else. Not such comforting words that would build a young boy's confidence and self-esteem, considering that I had lost those a long time ago.

The ranch had a very long driveway and I walked that to wait for the school bus. As the bus pulled up to pick me up, I very quickly got on and took the very first seat I could find and remained completely silent. I wanted to not mess up again and cause even more problems, which would most likely wind up with me getting into trouble with Robert.

As we got ready to arrive at the elementary school. I was terrified as to what might happen.

As I sheepishly got off the bus, and from that point on, the other boys, especially the jocks, would call me all kinds of names, strike me, and at times push me down into a puddle of water or mud.

They also told me very clearly that people like me do not belong there and that their parents would tell my foster parents about horrible things that I did not even do. School did not get off to a good start. And in that moment, I thought I had answered my own question—what is it with me that those boys instantly saw? What was wrong with me? I felt so ugly and so ashamed of my body. I just felt even more like trash.

I took the bus back home and thankfully the ranch was one of the last stops, so the name calling had subsided. I dreaded getting back to the house, in total fear that the other parents might have contacted Robert and Carolyn, like the boys threatened me with. With intent, I walked very slowly up that long driveway, having pictures in my mind of what could happen to me when I got home.

Surprisingly, when I did arrive at the house, Robert and Carolyn were waiting in the family room, and without even asking how my first day of school went, they told me that they had a gift for me. That gift turned out to be a beautiful Quarter Horse named "One Quarter".

I was so excited on the one hand, but my questioning mind was already concocting up bad or horrible things that could happen. Robert took me out to the stables, and for two days, he taught me how to take care of a horse, how to saddle it, to mount, using the guiding cords, and riding her.

He was very patient with me and I almost felt like we had made a connection. I took care of her, establishing a bond with her, and learning very quickly how to ride. She became a refuge for me after very bad school days with the name calling and the physical abuse having continued. I very much enjoyed riding and spending time with her; she became my best friend. I thought finally something is going well.

But riding her one day, the bit in her mouth somehow got stuck behind her teeth. Panicked, she went tearing off through the field with me on her. We were headed straight for a barbed wire fence surrounding the ranch. Just before we hit it, she bucked and threw me straight into it—barbed wire, boards, and wood. I felt as though I could barely move. Looking up, I could not find One Quarter and somehow managed to scrape myself together. I was in very wretched pain. Where I landed was a good distance back to the house, but somehow, I managed to get back to the house in an almost crawling position.

When I entered through the front door, there were Robert and Carolyn, who after taking a look at me, Carolyn gasped and asked what had happened. Before I could answer her, Robert started shouting at me, already accusing me of messing this up as well. Robert raged at me as to "how I could be so stupid and ignorant, unable to even control a Quarter Horse. What else do you expect to control in Your life? Just stupid."

The horse incident clearly showed my identify and where I stood with Robert, and with those very painful words, it left me questioning even more as to how I could possibly begin to love God, as by this time, my fatherly picture of Him took on that of my own father and foster father.

Carolyn did accompany me to the bathroom. She checked and helped me clean up. Fortunately, I was not hurt all that bad, other than my pride. She told me that she was sorry about what had happened, and she caressed me softly with her hand. She told me that there was not much she could do about Robert and that I should not tell him that she came to visit me. And so the secrets and deception began—never tell him anything. I figured that he must be passed out drunk somewhere in the house, otherwise she would not have had the courage to come and check up on me. I felt so isolated, so rejected. In that moment, this small gesture from a very passive foster mother meant something to me.

One Saturday morning, Robert told me at breakfast that he was taking me to get a haircut. I dared not question him and said, "Yes, Sir." That name was drilled into me by him, which meant to me, *do not respond with any other words.*

My hair was a bit longer and I had managed to have grown some light sideburns, for which I did mention to Robert at some point that I liked them very much. He did not respond.

When we entered the barber shop, Robert shook the barber's hand and whispered something into his ear, causing both men to look over at me chuckling. I did not think much about it, and the barber told me to get in the chair, which was fitted with a child raiser seat. He put the chair cloth on me and then got his clippers and scissors ready. I was high enough in the chair to see in the mirror that my foster father was seated behind us. The barber asked me if I would like to keep my sideburns. I said, "Yes, Sir, I would." In one fell swoop, he took a clipper in each hand, cut both sideburns off, and then handed them to me saying, "You said you wanted to keep them, right"? Immediately he and my foster father were laughing so hard and pointing fingers at me. I was so distraught but I knew that I could not cry or complain, because I knew what would happen if I did. It was humiliating.

I got down out of the chair and secretly held on to those one-time sideburns, something I was proud of. On the way home, Robert made some comment like, "We showed you." My answer should have been, "And yes, one day I will show you," but somehow, I remembered going to church and learning that the sixth commandment teaches us about honoring our parents.

Back home, I went to my room and began thinking how I could reattach the sideburns, but realized that this would not work, so I took them and hid them in the back of my scrapbook so that no one could ever take them away from me again. To this date, I still have them hidden away. When I do look at them, I have such vivid memories of that day, and then bad thoughts come towards my foster father, but I try not to dwell on that.

Most children might laugh off something like that, but to me, he took something that belonged to me, and like others had taken things from me before, including in that jail cell, this all just made me feel less and less like a person and more like trash, just an object.

After living with them for almost two years, Robert and Carolyn told me they were bringing in a new foster child. I dared not ask why or say anything. The boy, Randy, showed up one day. He had a terrible aura about him. Immediately, I could tell he didn't like me. It was mutual: we had become enemies without even exchanging a word. I was scared, the thought of sharing a room with another boy. The thoughts of what happened in jail came rushing back in. Up until this time, I told no one about what happened then. In fact, it took many years to tell someone what happened.

I had a single bed in my large bedroom. My foster parents placed a second bed; that that done, he was living with us.

On just his second day, (I could not sleep the first night he was there being in sheer terror that an assault might take place), I was in the living room watching TV. I was lying on the couch when, all of a sudden, complete darkness came over me. I couldn't breathe. He put a pillow over my head and said, "You're dead now, I hate Your guts."

I thought, *that's it, you're going to die here at young age. You'll asphyxiate and be gone.* But even stating earlier that I wanted to die, inwardly, I desperately called out to the God that Reverend Moore preached about that He will be with you and save you.

Fortunately, my foster mother who was in the open kitchen heard something was going on. She came in and tore him and the pillow off my face and pushed him away. I was able to start breathing again. It was so terrifying.

In a few hours he was gone. Even so, this traumatic experience stays with me to this date. So, was it God who answered that prayer? I pondered this thought for a long time.

In this story, I mentioned how I hated cement benches and the broom. To those, let me add pillows.

When Robert arrived later, he heard what had happened. He said, with these words that pushed me deeper into a downward emotional spiral, "Well, you must have brought it on Yourself. After all, you're nothing but trouble." I was beginning to start learning how to truly hate other human beings.

Even with this tragic event, they decided to take on other boys. With that, I wasn't alone anymore, and would not be again. The situation left me wondering what's going to happen next and who would try to kill me—and boy, it got even worse!

Three boys moved in within a few days of each other. I was the youngest. After very briefly introducing them to me, Robert told them to watch out for me because I am just trouble and not worth anything. So that is how I learned to view myself.

Two of the boys abused me, as well as an older boy whom my foster father hired to work on the ranch.

So, I wanted to just give up and just surrender. I had no strength; I had no power. I only wished it would all end, my life included.

It was bound to happen: one day, Robert caught me having sex with one of the older boys. He literally flew into an uncontrollable rage, pulled me by the hair off the bed, slapped me, and dragged me by my hair from my bedroom, through a hallway and into the family room. He picked me up until our faces were level, and he proceeded to punch me with all the force he could muster.

While at it, he said, "You know what, you little faggot? The only place that you're going to wind up is in hell!" (In that moment, I thought of other "pounding fists"—those of Reverend Moore).

With that, he punched me straight in my stomach. The force of that punch sent my body hurling through a huge bay window overlooking the swimming pool in our backyard.

I landed on the pool deck in a pile of broken glass. I was bleeding profusely and there was blood everywhere. All the while, I was in such excruciating pain.

It was devastating on so many levels. I hated him with great contempt. I wanted to get back at Robert for what he had done to me. I wanted him to feel the intense pain I was going through, but multiplied many times over.

But something inside me said, *Chase, forgive him, this too will pass. Revenge is not the answer.*

I pulled myself up on my knees and crawled back to a spare bedroom. The pain became even worse. I somehow managed to get into bed before passing out.

I woke up still covered in blood, with bruises and welts all over. This time Carolyn did not come. I was at rock bottom.

So, I wanted to just give up and surrender. I had no strength; I had no power. I only wished it would all end, my life included.

Robert acted like the violent episode never happened. But his treatment of me took on a different turn. He continually called me even worse and very degrading names, beating me at every opportunity he could find, and often for no reason at all. The beatings left me with multiple welts until they could no longer bring me anywhere with them. I was left home alone for the most part.

Shortly after, the other three boys were taken from the home—but why was I being left or not taken? I just wanted to scream out for help—anything or anyone. I just kept remembering what was said to me in that jail cell—"Keep Your mouth shut, or else." I was terrified of the "else."

But regarding church, Robert made sure that my arms were completely covered with long armed, oversized sweaters, and I was made to wear a large baseball cap so my entire face could not be seen.

I was forced to be there with them, and was told very clearly by Robert that I had better be on my best behavior and to put a smile on my face and act as though everything was fine, and that our family was a happy one. This was such a hard thing to do; on the inside falling apart, and on the outside, pretending that everything is perfectly normal.

I decided right then that my life called for a mask. So, I started wearing different masks to hide the pain. They conveniently allowed me to show people that everything was all right. But something was still off. I realized that the pain and the suffering I was living through far outweighed the coping resources that I had. It was awful.

I guess life kind of went on while I learned to hate myself even more.

Robert never stopped reminding me that going to hell was the only thing I was good for. He called me trash at times. And if I was trash to him, why did he keep me?

So, I remained in his house. So, I figured out how to wear the masks better. I needed to look good to other people, to please not only Robert but everyone. Nevertheless, they were just masks. Inside, I had no life, no anything, just hollow masks.

And so, I steeled myself to go on despite going through all the trauma and pain.

At least, there was something still working well for me—school. So, I put all the energy and resources I had into my studies. My reward was being at the top of my class.

The teachers liked me—they said I was an excellent student and writer. One day, our class was also offered a bit of comic relief, a form of reprieve even so fleeting for my sorry life.

It was in the fifth grade when one of the teachers provided one such moment. The teacher was Mrs. Hodgewell. She taught English. It was one of my favorite subjects and she one of my favorite teachers.

Mrs. Hodgewell was a very short and stout woman who was probably wider than she was tall. She had this habit of wearing high heels and tight dresses that made her look like "a packed sausage." It made me chuckle. In her classes, she always had a stepladder to help her draw level with the higher blackboard. One day, she climbed the stepladder as she always did.

It probably was not her day: while doing so, her dress just exploded as the seams broke open, flying all over in front of the chalkboard—leaving her with just her bra, girdle, and whatever else she had on. Yet, she took the event gracefully, dealing with it with her good sense of humor.

While I took in all the moment's hilarity, I also wondered if that was how women were supposed to look underneath, after seeing it for the first time. A new, but strange thought to me.

There was a very beautiful girl in my class, Teri, who went out of her way to befriend me, and she became what I thought would be a good friend.

One day, we went out and sat Indian style on the school playground. She told me that she sensed that there was something wrong and that if so, I could open up and talk to her about it. She held my hand. The rest of the world just stopped existing for me in that moment, and I thought, *why not, just open up to her and share the great pain inside of me*. I did just that, my first time opening up about a lot, with the exception of what happened in jail and the beatings. The two of us teared up. I felt that someone was connecting with me. It felt good.

And then she looked at me and, out of nowhere, said, "You know what, Chase…? Would you like to be my boyfriend? Do you want us to go together?"

I said yes in the hope that things could turn around and get better for me. It made me happy.

But sadly, we were together all of 57 minutes. I noticed that she had motioned to one of the school jocks to come over to us, he being the one who abused me the most. Teri then proceeded to tell him what I had opened up to her about. I could not believe what I was hearing—absolute betrayal. She turned to me and coyly said that I took her bait so easily and what a fool and loser I was. With that, she stood up, took the jock's hand, and told me that he was her boyfriend and they then walked off together. I was floored. I was devastated. And I thought to myself, *if only she knew what he had been doing to me the whole time.* I just kept my mouth shut. Trust became even harder for me after that.

Prior to the rape in jail and sexual abuses after, I vaguely remember a sermon about not having sexual relations before marriage. Taking it as crucial to the faith, I vowed even back then to keep myself a virgin until I married. Well, that didn't quite work out—it was robbed and stolen from me.

I formed an identity—I'm damaged goods anyway, trash, a waste of oxygen, unwanted, unloved, and no value to anyone.

With this, I questioned how a God would even think about wanting me? I felt rejected by Him as well.

At some point, I started becoming a habitual liar. I had to hide the truth about how wrong things were, instead telling everyone that everything's great, everything's perfect! How wrong that was!

Back then, there was really no research about why the lying had become so bad, almost an addiction. Today, it has a medical name, which is considered an illness—confabulation. I am, by no means, a medical expert, but from what I have read and researched, confabulation refers to the production or creation of false or erroneous memories without the overt intent to deceive, sometimes called "honest lying." In my upbringing in the church and with what the Bible teaches that honesty is virtuous, is there even such a thing? Or is it just evil?

Alternatively, confabulation can cause a falsification of memory by a person who has suffered huge trauma, whether physical, verbal, or sexual, and the person believes he or she is genuinely communicating truthful memories. With me, for example, I would tell people how great my childhood was, what loving wonderful parents and family I had, that we were well established and wealthy. Honest lying? At the time, it did make sense, albeit false, and so I convinced myself that it was okay. But inside I was plagued with so many other questions about my life – where to from here, what will happen next?

From as far back as I can remember, all I ever wanted was to get away—to flee, move, and go anywhere. I can't tell if it was plain wanderlust or just the need to flee from all those people who abused me so badly, or those who I had come to firmly believe didn't really want me.

I loved the water from a very early part of my life, taking a special interest in springboard, tower, and cliff diving.

In the summer of 1971, Robert told me that either I had to go to a YMCA camp in the mountains or he would just kick me out as he was just fed up with me. Had I become such a bad child and a burden to him? Having no other choice other than to be thrown out of his home, I chose to go to the summer camp. There, too, the abuse continued. It was terrible and agonizing. I kept saying to myself, *why does this continue to happen to me? Why don't they all just leave me alone?* But what kept me there was the program for cliff diving. I loved it, I loved the heights, and all that had to do with it.

The diving instructors told me that I had the kind of body (that surprised me as I had always been teased about my body) for this particular sport. I knew it was only a matter of getting those angles and twists right. I intently listened to their instruction and guidance.

I was able to flee the realities of the abuse awaiting me when I returned to camp, so I just practiced even harder and longer, staying each day until the last possible second. Well, I did learn those angles and twists. On the last day of camp, there was a diving competition.

I was prepared, I was pumped up. I gave it all I could, knowing that I had to get this perfect to get at least one thing right, and maybe get people applauding after I executed some difficult dives, and then ultimately them liking me.

The other competitors were not even in my mind. I solely focused the task at hand—to do this, and do it well. With each round, the applause became louder and more intense. And my competitive nature and overwhelming desire to finally succeed at something drove me to even more complicated and somewhat dangerous dives.

After the last round, the judges huddled together to vote. The air was thick with anticipation, and inside I was shaking.

They named the second and third place divers. And then for what seemed an eternity, it was announced that after receiving 10 points, a perfect score, from each of the judges, the first-place winner was me!

I could not believe what they said and that I had won! I was beside myself. I finally had done something good, something right.

I took much comfort from people liking my performance, and then the standing ovation. That afternoon, I took it as a form of acceptance. The feeling I got was simply exhilarating and phenomenal. Had I finally started a new path to success? I still have the first-place certificate in my scrapbook to this date!

After returning home, Robert showed no interest in my success, but Carolyn did tell me that I had done a good job, a first for her, and that after almost two years! I was floored that someone had said I had done a good job!

Carolyn told me that there was an envelope addressed to me on the table. I took it to my room and opened it. Inside was a birthday card from my parents, with a short-handwritten note wishing me a happy birthday. And in that note, was the first time they had called me son. I wept bitterly. If only I had heard that name so many years ago. I still have that card in my scrapbook. I looked at it several days ago, and wept once again. Both of my parents by then were long dead.

I worked on the farm bailing hay, cleaning the stalls, and taking part in the slaughtering of the animals. I just remember the great steaks produced from those cattle. They were huge, and wrapped in the old-style butcher paper. Carolyn marked each package with from which animal the meat came from, the date, and what cut it was. She did take the time to show me how to do this. She was, at times, a very loving person, but she was very passive and very much subservient, and almost, as it appeared, terrified of Robert, who, sadly, had also became an alcoholic, drinking in excess almost every day. So again, I just tried not to be there. The memories from my own father were just too painful—the nakedness and the strewn blood, and this repeating itself again! I wandered about the vast ranch, talking mostly to myself and just wondering what life was all about and started thinking more about God, whether He exists at all. I had been through so much trauma at this point that I doubted a God who takes delight in me, wants me to forgive and love as He does, would even exist. With all that had happened, this was all foreign to me. I remember thinking how could He even allow this.

I did take some comfort, even at that young age, from reading about the great sufferings that many people experienced in the history of the Bible. I was somewhat comforted that bad things happen to other people, but for me, being at such a young age, I concluded that I did not want to continue on with this degree of suffering, all considered. I concluded that perhaps I am not "salvageable," basically trash as I had so often been made to believe. It was very difficult for me to process while traipsing around some 10,000 acres of land, sometimes shouting at the top of my voice, "Why?"

Just prior to the 1972 Summer Olympics, in Munich, Germany, we acquired a television. We had to use aluminum foil to roll into balls, stick them on the ends of the rabbit ears, and move around until we could see something.

I was sitting in front of the television when they showed the springboard and tower diving events. The pictures were fuzzy, but right there and then, I told myself I'm going to dive in that very same place, the Munich Olympic Pool. I didn't know how or when I would make it to Germany from the United States, but I knew that not only would I accomplish this, but that Germany would be my ultimate home!

After being hurled through that bay window, the hate and abhorrence from my foster father grew stronger.

He drank excessively almost every day. He would tell me, over and over again, that I was worth absolutely nothing and that I would surely land in hell. At one point, he screamed that if I did not die first, he would help me get there. I thought for the first time that he would actually follow through with this threat. I was so terrified of him that I tried to stay out of his way as much as possible.

And so I poured myself into school, studying harder and harder and always looking to take on extra assignments in all of my subjects to keep me occupied, trying as hard as I could not to think of what could come next with Robert.

I attained academic excellence at school, receiving praises and accolades from my teachers, and also received an outstanding achievement award. Here, in addition to diving, I knew that at least I was good at something.

The hardest part of it all came when we had class tests. The jocks—the same ones who abused me terribly needed good grades in order to remain on the sports teams—threatened to tell on me if I did not help them prepare for the tests. They would also try their best to sit next to me during tests.

It was hard because there was no one I could trust to talk to about what's going on. Even worse was having my abusers sitting next to me. It was so gut-wrenching thinking of the horrible things they did to me, and then using me to get the grades they needed.

Sometimes, I felt like exposing them for what they were, but with my horrible upbringing and all, who would even believe me? I just kept the mask on.

One of my last memories of that school involved the school yearbook. There were drawings of a boy and a girl next to each other, and the title over each drawing was "dream boy" and "dream girl." Funny thing, Teri was the one who put that together. She named different boys and girl for each body part that would make up the perfect "dream boy or girl." Her boyfriend, who had abused me, was named for the muscles; the other boys who had abused me were named for the hair, the smile, the face, the legs, fingers, etc. One boy, me, was singled out for the left toe. It did not hurt me so much in that I was named for the toe, but because I had suffered from fungus on that toenail as long as I could remember. It triggered me, even to this day when I look back at that yearbook. Just fungus!

Back at the ranch, the verbal and physical abuse continued, often erupting into great attacks from Robert.

Carolyn would stand there and watch it all happening, doing nothing. When he was so drunk, I believe she was also very afraid of him.

In one particularly violent situation, Robert lost all control. He was screaming at me, telling me that I was just trash and a loser.

I felt so worthless and unwanted. It left me silently calling out to God that I needed help.

That answer, perhaps, did come in the form of a strong nudging to just flee and get out of there. I was almost seventeen at that point. After experiencing this abuse for almost six years, I decided to get out.

I waited for an opportune moment when my foster parents were not there. I grabbed my backpack with just a few items in it and went out the front door. I looked back at the place that was full of hate, rejection, abuse, and yes, abandonment. I said to myself in that very moment, *it is done, over.*

Once I got to the end of the driveway, I started to run, to run as fast as I could to escape, to get out of there.

The ranch was in the country. The nearest town was where my school was located, for which I always had to take the bus to. I just ran.

After putting physical distance between me and that place, I was out of breath. I started walking.

There was a trail just to the right of the road that was surrounded by trees, so I kept myself hidden while walking there. I did not want to be found.

Then I started to think about where I should go. I felt so alone, but I knew I needed to go somewhere. My parents' house was some two-and-a-half hours by car from the ranch. I decided that for whatever reason, that is where I would go.

I started questioning in my mind what would happen when I got there. Would Robert and Carolyn report me as missing and that the police would track me down? Would I then be put into that juvenile hall again or a fate even worse?

I walked and walked.

At some point, a car pulled over to the side of the road. The driver rolled down the window and asked me where I was going. I told her I wanted to go to my parents' house. I told her where that was and she said she was headed in that direction and offered to give me a ride. I got into her car.

I was very cold and immediately felt the warmth of the car heating system. The lady introduced herself to me.

Her name was Kathy, who I guessed would have been around fifty years old. She had a bottle of chocolate milk that she offered to me. I said thank you and drank it.

We drove in silence for what seemed to be a good while, until she started talking.

She said that she was returning home from a church retreat in the mountains. My first thought was, *not again, more church?*

Would she sense that something was wrong with me and that her reaction would be to start talking about salvation?

I braced myself by tensing my body, preparing for the worse.

To my surprise, Kathy was very gentle and told me that I looked like I had been through a lot and that I did not have to talk about why I was alone on foot so far out in the country.

She started talking about her church retreat and what a big blessing it was to her and that she felt the presence of God for the first time in a long time.

She then shared some of her life story, which also included abuse, rejection, and abandonment. The more she spoke, the more I started to relax.

She had been through a lot, and in that moment, I felt like I was not alone in what happened to me.

She told me that during the retreat, which was for people who had experienced severe abuse, the counselors talked about the love of God and how unconditional it was, that nothing could separate us from his love, not tribulation, distress, persecution, famine, nakedness, or danger.

I remembered from church and also reading in my Bible that she was referring to Romans 8:35. I mentioned this to her.

She said that those verses in Romans 8 stated said that we are more than conquerors and that neither death nor life, nor angels nor rulers, nor things to come, nor height nor depth, nor anything else in all creation (and here she added that this included the abuse she experienced from her husband) would ever be able to separate her from the love of God.

She said that she had struggled for so long and could not tell anyone about it as her husband was a church leader and otherwise had a very "good and clean" Christian reputation, but that during the church retreat, she broke down and told her story.

She made the decision to bring it into the open and expose his behavior. She did say that through all of this, forgiveness was a central theme at the retreat, and that at some point, she decided to forgive him.

My heart went out to her and I remember telling her that she was very brave in doing what she did. It relaxed me somewhat and I begin to start thinking if I should consider doing the same thing.

She sensed that something was wrong, and very tenderly told me that if there was anything I wanted to talk about, I could do that with her. But in that moment, my mind returned to the school yard incident with Teri and so many other betrayals, and said to myself that I would not trust again so quickly.

I did thank her for her concern and shrugged it off by saying that it would be fine. She seemed to accept that.

The drive went by quickly. When we approached the town where my parents lived, I asked her if I could be left off at the freeway exit.

As we pulled over to the side of the road, she said to me that life just gets messed up very badly at times, but she sensed that I was a fighter and that whatever was going on with me, I would continue on with the fight. She told me that without a doubt, God would do mighty things in my life, He would bless me greatly, and that He was with me and that He had special plans for me. (What special plans that it would all end horribly?)

She got out of the car and said, "I do not know what Your hurt is, but I know hurt, and so does the Lord." She asked if she could give me a hug. I told her yes and she gave me the sweetest hug I had experienced in my life. At that moment, I felt a real and true warmth from another human being.

She released me from that hug and told me that she would be praying for me, and then said something that struck me oddly, "We just might see each other again. God knows what He is doing." As she waved and drove away, I thought to myself that just maybe there is a God and that nothing could separate me from His love. And then Cathy telling me that we might see other again, and that God knows what He is doing, provided just a shimmering bit of hope for me.

But I was still troubled with the notion that I deserved everything that happened to me. And instead of heeding those words from Cathy, I chose the negative, and I came to the conclusion that God had decided to curse me, a curse from which I could not come back from.

In later adult years, I would be told by Christian counselors that because I was told about family's and so-called generational sins (how they knew that I do not know), God might be punishing me based on those iniquities, as stated in Exodus 34:6-7, Deuteronomy 5:5-10, and Leviticus 26:39.

And I accepted and believed that I was cursed and that there would be no chance to make it right with God.

That was terrifying to me, and only fell into line with what I had been told so many times—that I would ultimately go to hell.

As I walked the streets of that town where so much bad happened—finger pointing, name calling, abuse, rejection, and abandonment—my mind was reeling. I was not sure if I wanted to experience this; not just here, but never again.

As I entered the driveway to my parents' house, I climbed the front porch steps where my father had passed out so many times from being drunk, lying in pools of blood from the bad falls he took.

I thought to myself, *what brought me back here?* I was not sure that this was where I wanted to be, but for whatever reason, here I was. It had been a long trip and I was tired and exhausted.

I knocked at the door, and my mother answered the door. She just looked at me in disgust and asked me what in the hell I was doing back there, and what had I screwed up this time. If she only knew.

She then left the door hanging and went back inside. I fought with myself about what to do, but I thought maybe it would be better this time, in spite of her very cruel words. I knew in that moment that I was not welcome there.

And that knowledge proved to be right. After I entered the house, she had already sat back down at the table and was playing solitaire, a favorite game of hers.

Without even asking what had happened, she blurted out that since I was there, I might as well stay there and finish out my high school years. The only other thing she said was she would have to talk to the authorities, but followed that statement up by telling me that I had better straighten up and toe the line; if not, even worse things would happen. (How many times had I heard that statement?) My thought in that moment was, *what could "even worse" be?* My second thought went back to the moment of opening that birthday card and being addressed as son, and now getting yelled at. Why in the hell was I back there again? I was very mixed up.

As I shared from my childhood, I hated Friday nights because of my father. And I hated Fridays as that night was when football games and school dances took place. Also, there was a hangout spot not far from my parent's home. This is where the popular kids would meet together. I could hear them in the distance, along with the voices of those who abused me while pretending they were the coolest of the cool.

I sometimes wish I would have found the courage to go there and confront them with what they had done to me, but I could not. Something was holding me back. It was very hard and those deep scars of torment are still with me today. I did not think they would ever completely go away, and here I was only seventeen years old.

At home, things turned to worse one Friday evening when my older brother came home drunk. We shared a room. I woke up to his noisy entrance. My mother was gone and my father was passed out drunk in his room. I tried to ask my brother to be quiet, at which point he became very aggressive and started calling me those same names that I have heard so many times: gay, queer, sissy, etc.

I asked him to stop but he became even more aggressive. He came over to my bed and said, "Shut up! I will show you what happens to fairies like you!" He then pressed me face down on my back and made me give him oral sex. I tried to fight him off, but like in jail so many years ago, he held my hands behind me.

It was horrible. I thought, *this is my brother, how could this be happening?* After he finished, he released my arms, punched me in my stomach, and told me that if I ever said anything, he would kill me.

In that moment, I wanted to tell him to go ahead and kill me. It would have been much better for me to be dead than alive.

These acts happened several times. I hated him and had real thoughts of killing him. With my anger and fantasy, it would not have been a pleasant death for him. My brother would take his own life years later. But I just could not bring myself to say or do anything. I do remember saying to God that my life could not get any better and that if He cared for me, He would intervene and do something.

He did not then and this time not again. I had really become just a disposable object to others—just as I was back then so many times referred to as—trash. And so thoughts of ending my own life moved more to the forefront of my mind.

And then, one day, my younger sister told me that she had a friend who liked me and that she was interested in going to the senior prom with me. My immediate response was absolutely not and out of the question. But my sister persisted and told me that it would be okay.

Very reluctantly, I agreed. This would be the very first date I went on, and her name was Linda, a very nice-looking girl, very sweet, very tender. She interested me because she, too, was not well liked (or so I thought), and she had very good grades at school.

So, I decided to purchase a suit for the prom, a baby blue polyester suit, which was, in those days, very modern and popular.

My thoughts turned back to Robert, of him saying he would make a man out of me. So, I swallowed the thought that when I did show up at the prom, it would not be a good thing. But I had to try and prove Robert right. I was on a mission.

I also purchased a corsage for Linda and was able to borrow my mother's car for the evening. I drove to Linda's house and picked her up. She looked very beautiful in her pretty white dress. I thought that this might just turn out to be okay.

On the way to the school for the prom, Linda casually told me that she had a boyfriend, that they had just broken up and that she just needed to be with someone on this what she called a special evening, and that was why she spoke to my sister about me as I would "prove to be harmless."

I immediately thought to myself that this situation did not look like it would go in a good direction and in that moment, I considered just turning around and take her home. But Robert's words flooded in. I steeled myself and resolved to see this through, regardless of the outcome. When I look back at it now, I wish I had turned around, took Linda home, and then just disappeared somewhere.

Yet I had seen on television or in magazines how senior proms looked and it piqued my curiosity. When we arrived at the high school, there was valet parking, and I stopped the car. My understanding of valet parking is that the valet would open the door for you to get out and that they park Your car.

The valet waiting just happened to be one of my greatest abusers since returning back to my parents' home. When we locked eyes, it was like an eternity had passed. All of the abuse that I went through him just raced through my mind. I was frozen in place; I could not move. When I came back into reality, I saw that teachers and chaperones were present, and that, I supposed, precluded him from a verbal attack. I did see that he was whispering into another student's ear and then, with a pointed finger, cackling in my direction.

Linda asked me what was going on. I lied and said I did not know. I realized there would be no valet service in that moment, so I made a quick decision to drive the car myself to the parking lot. I knew that something horrible was getting ready to happen, but I just pressed on.

I got out of the car, went around, and opened the door for Linda, who surprisingly, seemed to be unfazed by what was happening. We walked the short distance to the entrance to the building, entered the room together, and it did not take me long to see how fast the news traveled from that whisper and finger pointing outside to that moment.

As soon as we walked into the door, every head turned, especially the boys who had had their way with me. They started laughing and just making fun of me, saying things like "What, he really is with a girl," and "What is trash like him doing here?"

There were cat calls and comments like, "Go home! You do not belong here; you are just trash!" One of the chaperons took pity on me and tried to reassure me that we should stay there and that it would be okay. I just wanted to turn around and run, and at twice the speed at which I had fled from my foster parent's home. It was humiliating.

We were placed at a table in the far back corner, next to the kitchen and the bathrooms, totally separated from the rest of the other guests. Linda had become somewhat agitated at this point, and when I asked her what was wrong, she reacted with telling me that we would just go and dance. Instinctively, I knew, that something was wrong, and that something terribly wrong was about to happen. Why did I just not flee? All I did was just put on another mask.

I do not ever remember dancing in my life, and so as we approached the dance floor, I was struck by looking up at the banner over the stage with the theme of the senior prom: Highway to Hell, a song by AC/DC (I had to ask myself, *What is that for a senior prom theme, was that selected extra for me?*) At that point, so many things raced through my mind. Seeing that banner took me back to the past with my mother and others on so many occasions times telling me how I was headed for hell, and those fiery sermons warning unrepentant sinners of going to hell for eternity. I believed I was on that highway, like a high-speed eighteen-wheeler truck smashing into a solid cement wall. That would definitely lead to total destruction and maybe fulfill what I thought were prophesies told about me.

Back to the dance floor, I was sweating profusely knowing that I would now be fully exposed and "on stage" in front of the whole senior class. As we approached the dance floor, that song just happened to start playing.

On the dance floor and in a bit of a larger crowd, I tried to pretend that no one else was there, once again slipping into a world that had only existed to me. I tried to reassure myself that it would all be okay, and as I slowly began to move my legs to the music, which had felt like they had been cemented to the floor. I began to think that we might just go unnoticed. I tried to relax and just close my eyes and tried to sway with the music.

For what seemed like an eternity, I had my eyes closed, and found myself thinking that I might not be doing too bad here. Then I heard laughing and cackling, and slowly opened my eyes. What I realized was that I was dancing alone. Linda was no longer there, and the entire senior prom attendees had formed a circle around me, laughing and pointing fingers, calling me all kinds of horrible names. I just wanted to rip open the dance floor and crawl underneath it.

Then I noticed Linda also standing there, staring at me and laughing, and then someone approached her and looked like they were whispering something into her ear, first pointing a finger at me and then into another direction. At that point, for the second time, Linda appeared to become very nervous and agitated. I was confused, as I thought she was my date, that she was on my side.

I stood there frozen in place, gripped with a terror that had overcome me, just sensing that something terrible was about to happen. Trying to drown out the loudness of the circle of the classmates that had formed a circle around me, I looked to Linda and tried to motion for help, but I could not move. After seeming like this would never end, the crowd started to dissipate. I was left standing in that same spot, with Linda starting to approach me.

When she did come to me, she casually reminded me that she had earlier told me that she had broken up with her boyfriend, thought it was over, but he did not think it was over, and he wanted her back. I quickly found out what the whispered message was. Linda informed me he was on his way to the dance after finding out she was there and there with me, whom he called a no one and just trash. She then very nervously told me that he was very jealous and that when very angry, he would most likely become physically violent.

Linda then took me by my arm, and we quickly proceeded to a back door, with me thinking, *what is going on here?* and *What will go wrong now?* The car was not too far from that entrance. Linda told me we need to run quickly, get into the car, and get out of there.

I quickly got Linda into the car and then got in myself and started it. In my mind, I was quickly going over the options, whether to just hightail it out of there or just drive out at a normal speed, in order to not attract any unwanted attention. I chose the second option and asked Linda if I should take her home. She said no and that she was afraid that he might be there waiting for her, but that he would be really waiting for me. She said she was so afraid due to his over possessiveness and he might try to physically harm me, even possibly try and kill me.

My thoughts were racing and was wondering if in fact, that could happen. Would I die on this evening, and if so, could this wind up being my "highway to hell!?" in lieu of the eighteen-wheeler scenario?

We proceeded to drive and Linda said she knew a closed alley way just ahead and we should pull into there. I said OK and I thought to myself that maybe this would be a good hiding place and stopped there and turned the car off. As we were sitting there, Linda had become even more nervous, looking out of the back window, and was crying and then started to scream. Feeling badly for her, I reached over to try and take her in my arms and hold her.

As I did that and try to ask her what was wrong, lo and behold, a car pulled in behind us with its bright lights on. I was blinded to see what kind of a car it was and who was in it. I quickly locked the doors.

It did not take very long to find out who it was, as from the passenger side of the car, a male appeared, who turned out to be her boyfriend, who I quickly recognized as another classmate who had abused me since returning to finish high school here.

I did not know he was Linda's boyfriend. He tried to open the door and was pounding with his fists on the window, calling me all kinds of names, and also with guttural threats as to what he was going to do with me once he had me in the grip of his hands.

As so many thoughts were ravaging through me, my first thought was how to protect Linda from her very jealous boyfriend, and so I turned to her to ask her if she was okay and what I could do to help. Her countenance quickly changed from what appeared to be nervousness and fear, to a very stone-cold face, at which point she turned to me and told me to get out of the car quickly. Why would she say that to me and not be thinking of herself. I quickly discovered she was. Her boyfriend was still on her side of the car. She casually rolled the window down and spoke very quietly to him. I thought she was trying to calm him down.

Linda opened her door and got out of the car, and then proceeded to say to him, "OK, he is delivered to you as you asked. Just do Your job and make it end quickly." Once again, a setup and an absolute betrayal.

And then she turned back to me and bent down into the car compartment and said to me, "Trash like you need to be mutilated and destroyed." She also confessed that this schoolmate was not her boyfriend; he was the end goal for the other classmates, with Linda's help, for what turned out to be a well-planned ambush and attack.

I tried to reason with Linda. I told her that I thought she was my friend. If so, how could she do this to me?

Before she could answer, he climbed into the car from her side, grabbed me, and dragged me out of the car, threw me to the ground and began punching me and jumping into the air, either landing on me with his feet by throwing the full weight of his body onto mine. All the time, he was telling me that he was going to kill me and that the world would be just done with me. I was so in shock that all I could do was try to shield the blows with my hands.

The attack continued for what seemed an eternity, and by that time, I had lost almost all feeling in my body. With one more huge blow from him, I lost consciousness. When I came to, it was just starting to get light, so I figured I had been lying there for a while. With the searing pain racing through my entire body, I noticed I was in a pool of blood. I thought, *What, blood again?* I was in shock, but I knew there would be no help coming, so after lying there for a while, I managed to crawl up on all fours, and what was the first thing I saw? Lying beside me was the corsage I had given to Linda, now covered in my own blood.

I thought of so many things, including my own sister. Had she been part of this whole scheme? I dismissed that thought as I could not believe she knew. And as passive as I was, I never asked her.

I managed to get back into the car. I had just been beaten to a pulp, verbally attacked to no end. As I leaned again the car door to find support, I remember saying to myself that I just cannot take any more of this. My body had been so abused by this point, my mind so mixed up, and my very soul was ravaged. And where was anyone, including God? Not there.

I remember there was a rope in the car. Even in much excruciating pain, and covered in blood and dirt, I managed to get to the passenger side of the car, reached in, and took the rope out. My thoughts went back to what all I had learned about tying knots at the summer camps that Robert and Carolyn had sent me to. I did not get back in the car because of the blood. I knew what would await me if I came back home with blood in the car.

I made the decision right then; this was it, my body could take no more. I wanted out, I did not want to be here any longer. There was absolute quiet and stillness in that alley. From my perspective, it was just the car, me, the bloodied corsage, and the rope. I realized, in that moment, I was already tying the knots and forming what would become a noose.

I knew that from where I was, *it* was not very far from where I was; my favorite "hiding" field where I would otherwise go and escape Friday nights. I found a blanket in the car. I spread it over the driver's seat so that it would not get bloodied up. Somehow, and mustering every last bit of strength I had, I managed to drive to a side street close to my parents' house and parked.

I then managed to get to the field where my favorite tree was, where I used to climb up to escape everything. It was a very majestic oak. That tree, if it had the capacity to understand, would know everything about me more than anyone else. I spent countless hours pouring my heart out to it, thinking that it would respond. In some way, I thought it did. I had, more than two years earlier, carved initials into the trunk of that tree, "IWDH." They were not my initials; instead, they stood for "I will die here."

I remember crying and started thinking about whether what I thought was a prophecy would be fulfilled here: *You are trash and trash needs to be destroyed, and then you will be on Your way to hell.*

I took the rope and somehow managed to shimmy up to my favorite branch and secured the rope there. And so, I took the noose and placed it around my neck, saying to myself that this is it. I had read about hanging and how it could happen very quickly, snapping Your neck and instantly dying. My thoughts began racing as to what I had done that was so awful and abominable, and the shame and guilt of those actions had become too much and why so many people said I was a loser, just trash. I made up my mind right there.

I took the rope and placed it around my neck. Surprisingly, I was not very afraid. I thought of the people who had told me that trash must be destroyed; I concluded to just annihilate it here.

I managed to crawl off onto the tree trunk, holding onto it with my hands, which were also in severe pain, and lowering my fragile and small body down as far as my arms would allow—as always, on a mission. And then I just let go of the branch and the rope, my full weight suspended in midair.

I had thought by researching that suicide by hanging would go quickly, your femur bone would break, and you would asphyxiate and die. But as I hung there, nothing happened other than my body gently swinging back and forth. My next thought was that if this hanging were to succeed, from a Biblical standpoint, this would, in effect, be murder, and that in not being able to confess this sin, I would not go to Heaven.

Why I had that thought, I do not really know, but then my thought turned back to the theme of the senior prom, Highway to Hell. I wondered which might happen: God, whom I did not really care for, would forgive me, and if not, would the devil make wide open the doors to eternal damnation? Lots to think about when you are suspended by a rope.

I hung there for what seemed a long time, and I thought to myself that I cannot even get this right. Then, for whatever reason, I begin to cry out for help, from anyone or anything. It was as though time stood still.

And then the weirdest thing happened. The rope, which I had made into a noose and thought would do the trick, just literally tore in two and my body was let loose, but it felt as though as I was floating to the ground, a good 15-foot drop. When I landed and, in a daze, my first thought was, *why did this not work? Why am I still here?* More crucially, *Who or what helped me?*

And yes, I started yelling at God and berating Him for saving me from this; if indeed it was Him.

And still lying there, the next thing I saw was the bloody corsage that I had also taken with me after the attack—why? Good question; I still ponder that at times. I kept a small, bloodied flower petal that has been in my scrapbook to this date. I look at it from time to time. Every time I looked at it, I just thought so much about the pain, and it was as if I was reliving that incident and could actually feel some of that pain.

In any event, I concluded that this is just one more failure in a life filled with so many of them, and a life to come that might be filled with even more. At some point, it would have to end one way or another.

And my thoughts turned back to Robert. Why could I just not prove him right? I would never become a man. Perhaps, I should have chosen Carolyn's option after all.

I still was in a lot of pain from the attack, and probably sustained more after the fall, but I managed to get myself together, clean myself up with water from the nearby canal, and went back to the car, drove it to my parents' house, and parked. It was night time and there were no lights on, so I removed the towel and managed to go inside and go to bed, even with all that pain. But being so used to pain, it just did not seem to make matters worse, nor did anyone ask the next day. I masked the pain and covered the wounds. It was though I was invisible. But I remember Cathy telling me that I was a fighter.

After the events of the senior prom and the attempt to take my life, I dreaded returning to school. I knew what would come and what would be said, but I also knew that I needed to finish high school so I could finally escape and try to begin anew.

I used to walk to school every morning. One of our neighbors had a beautiful Alaskan malamute dog. I absolutely love dogs and she was so adorable. She was fenced in the yard and I looked forward each morning, to stop and pet her. I had been doing this for quite a long time. On that particular morning, already dreading the day ahead, as usual, I went by and on that day, which I had not witnessed before, the gate was open and she was sitting there and appeared to be happy to see me.

This time, she was not closed in. I knelt down to pet her and, all of a sudden, she jumped up and bit me on the bottom of my face from the nose down. She then ran back into the yard. Blood was pouring out profusely and I was in great pain, adding to the pain from the Friday before. My first thought was about the blood and going back to those horrific experiences where I had bled so much. Why, why, always with blood?

I grabbed my school bag and placed both hands on my face to try and stop the bleeding. I headed back home, leaving a trail of blood behind me.

When I got back home and entered, my mother was sitting at the table, as always, counting the money in the coffee cans. She did not notice me until I told her that I had been bitten. I thought she would be raging mad, but surprisingly, she asked me what happened. I told her and she grabbed several towels and told me to press them against my face. She then told me to wash my hands where so much blood was, and then she told me to get in the car.

The drive to the hospital was around 30 minutes, but seemed to take much longer. My mother did manage to ask me at one point how I was doing, and I lied and told her that I was okay, masking the pain. It did touch me, though, that she asked about how I was doing, probably hearing this from her for one of the first times in my life. Other than that, the drive was silent.

When we arrived at the hospital, I was immediately taken into the emergency room where the doctor looked at me and said that with the amount of blood I had lost, I should count myself lucky to be alive.

My thought was, *I wish I had died from this*. I did not want to be here any longer and then that haunting question that I had asked myself so many times before came to mind—*Just who am I?* This time, I mentally answered that question myself—*They were all right, and maybe even God, I am just junk*. With those thoughts, and from losing so much blood, I passed out on the examining table.

I regained consciousness at some point and found that I was alone in the hospital room. I thought that history tends to repeat itself. Seeing that my mother was not there, this time I did not even question why. I raised my hands to my face and realized that I could not touch it as it was heavily bandaged from my nose downwards. I managed to get out of bed. I went to the mirror and was shocked to see that it looked like someone had taken two objects, each about the size of tennis ball, and had bandaged them to my lower face. It was a ghastly sight. I did not want to think what my face looked like under all of that bandaging.

I called for the nurse, and she came with the doctor and my mother. The doctor described the process of the treatment, also telling me that they had to transfuse new blood into my body due to the amount of blood I had lost.

Here, I thought, I had lost so much blood in my short lifetime, and yes, also what I had not recorded here until now, the blood that I lost from Chuck's attack and from the other boys, or from the beatings and being hurled through that bay window. And now here I am getting someone else's blood?

My mind went back to Sunday School learning about how Jesus shed His blood for us and that through His shed blood, we had new life in Him. I remember hoping and praying, for whatever reason, that the blood came from Him, healing blood, new life. Knowing full well it did not, I just returned to wondering who gave their blood. Always wondering, always thinking, even in situations like this where I was in very real pain.

After a final checkup, I was released midafternoon. The drive home was mostly silent, other than my mother shouting at other drivers, as they were hindering her from getting home to watch *Jeopardy*. That made me very sad, and in this very hard time, it showed me where my place was in her heart.

We returned home at around noontime. I collapsed into bed and slept until the next morning. Even with all that happened, all I wanted to do was to get back to school as we were preparing for a very important final test in U. S. Government, a subject I enjoyed very much. I told my mother that after lunch, I would be heading back to school, receiving no response. I walked to school passing the place where the dog had lived. She was not there this time. I found out later that the authorities had come to pick her up to check for rabies, but by that time, the supposed owners had removed her. It was subsequently learned that they had stolen the dog, which was a champion show animal. I never heard anything about her again.

When I arrived at the classroom, the lesson had already begun. For some reason, I did not think about the heavy bandaging on my face, and when I walked in, there were glaring stares, followed by finger pointing, roaring laughter, and awful comments. One classmate even said, "Look at that mask he is wearing, and it is not even Halloween."

A mask? I asked myself. Even my favorite teacher joined in a bit with the other students. To say I was devastated is a great understatement. But this event did spare me the heckling and the awful comments that might have come about from the senior prom on Friday night. And funny, no comments or cajoling occurred again about the senior prom event.

A few days later, the bandages were removed and the stitches taken out. I dreaded seeing the results of that bite. The doctor commented that he had done the best he could, as I had multiple tears below my nose and around my mouth. The nurse asked me if I wanted to see how the operation went. I reluctantly said yes and she handed me a mirror. I immediately knew that scars would be permanent, and what I saw just devastated me. The outward right side of my lips were gone, leaving a sag. The wounds below my mouth required many more, longer stitches. It made me feel even more ugly, and my thought was why did the noose have to break? I would have these outward scars for the rest of my life, which are visible to all, but the inward and very horrible scars no one would see. I got teased about this a lot at school, and in other places. I just swallowed those comments.

One day, I was sitting in the shade of what I thought was my favorite tree, just kind of being mad at it because the hanging did not work. I had a log there. I was looking at my scars in a small handheld mirror. I thought I was alone, because never did I see anyone come by in all the times I had been there.

All of a sudden, I realized an older lady was standing next to me, seeming to come out of nowhere. A very grandmotherly-looking woman, she saw my face and asked me what had happened. I very reluctantly told her (I did not know why I told her at the time as I had lost so much trust with other people—I would find out why much later). She gently told me that everything would be okay, try to accept it, and encouraged me to put a smile on my face.

What? I thought to myself, *everything would be okay and put a smile on my face? No way that was going to happen.*

She said that God loves me not because of the outward appearance, but that He looks at the inward, the heart, and there she told me that in His eyes, I am wonderfully made just as I am. She said that she sensed that I had a very hard life, and she told me that even with all of that, He still has plans for me, to help me and not harm me, and that he would give me a future. She said that God would never leave me and never forsake me. I told her, "Thank you," and pretended to smile.

She gently approached me and asked if she could touch my face. I immediately tensed up, but reluctantly allowed her to. That was the first time anyone had touched those scars. Her hand was very warm and it felt good on my skin, not like the pain from all of the beatings and slaps to my face.

We made eye contact with each other (it felt so warm and real) and she said, "God will be with you when you are born again (I thought, *Oh no, not that verse again?*) and accept Jesus as Your Lord and Savior. He will wipe away every tear and heal you. Remember these words." She then encouraged me to read Psalm 139, to know just how much God knows and cares for me. I placed my hand on hers and it was so warm, so comforting, nothing like I had felt before. I just wanted to stay here with her warm hand on my face. I felt wanted and safe. And then she said to me "God bless you, child."

I had my eyes closed and was trying to take in everything that she said to me. When I opened my eyes, she was gone. I lowered my hand from my face and thought, *who was that? Was I imagining things?*

I then thought back to the ride that Cathy had given me. It reminded me so much of what this older lady had just told me. Could it have been that her and Cathy were angels as well? I do not know, but it felt strange to me.

I sat there contemplating all that she had told me. I had a backpack and I remember having a Bible in it (the Bible was given to me at summer camp several years before, and I remember throwing it in the backpack just before I fled from Robert and Carolyn). I do not know why I kept it in my backpack all this time. There were occasions where I wanted to just throw it away, but I never did. I removed it from my backpack. The book still had the light, smoky smell from summer camps at night when we sat around a huge fire and the counselors would read to us (I would try to follow along); it took my mind back to those days.

I started to just flip the pages, thinking about what we learned in Sunday school about the Bible.

I sat there for what seemed like many hours flipping through the pages trying to find a verse that backed up each statement that the older lady had said to me.

It was an exhausting search, and here is my journal entry from that day. Usually, I would write paragraphs, but on this occasion, I listed these verses:

1 Samuel 16:7 "For the LORD sees not as man sees: man looks on the outward appearance, but the LORD looks on the heart."

John 3:3 "Jesus answered him," Truly, truly, I say to you, unless one is born again, he cannot see the kingdom of God."

Psalm 139:14

"For I am fearfully and wonderfully made."

Jeremiah 29:11-12 "For I know the plans I have for you, declares the LORD, plans for welfare and not for evil; to give you a future and hope. Then you will call upon me and come and pray to me, and I will hear you."

Deuteronomy 31:8

"It is the LORD who goes before you. He will be with you; *He* will not leave you or forsake you. Do not fear or be dismayed."

And I thought to myself once again, *what just happened?* I took a well-deserved break. I laid the open Bible next to me on the log. There was a light breeze blowing. As the Bible lay open, the breeze blew and turned the pages. The breeze abruptly stopped. For some reason, I looked down at the Bible and it was open to Hebrews Chapter 13.

So I begin reading the chapter, but was stopped cold very early in that chapter, in verse two, which states, "Do not neglect to show hospitality to strangers, for thereby some have entertained angels unawares."

That verse struck me as, like I said, when I opened my eyes, the older lady was gone. Could she have been an angel? I did not even believe in something like this, and certainly had not thought about it before.

I pondered that thought for a while and then continued and came to verses 5 and 6, "I will never leave you nor forsake you." And we can confidently say, "The Lord is my helper; I will not fear; what can man do to me?"

I thought, *My helper?* I questioned where was He when all of the abuse and violence was happening. Why did He not step in and put a stop to it? After all, I was just a boy.

And then I thought about the rest of the verse, "What man can do to me?" So I opened a new page in my journal and started to write out names of people who I listed and what they did to me:

Mother - Explosive anger, physical and verbal abuse, showing no love. By the way, it hurts me to put this down in writing, but she was naked most of the time at home, and would always make me rub her back and pop her pimples while she watched *Jeopardy*—I hated that immensely.

Father - Drunk, aloof, uncaring

Sister - Did she connive with Linda?

Brother – Drunk; sexual and verbal abuse

Chuck - The beginning of it all—rape, verbal abuse, threats

Robert - Drunk, a drillmaster, verbal, physical, and great psychological abuse, explosive anger, threats

Carolyn - Very passive, her desire was to have a girl and tried to steer me in this direction

Randy - Tried to kill me by asphyxiation

Teri - Deceptive; set me up by pretending to be my girlfriend

School jocks—Sexual, verbal, and physical abuse

Linda - Deceptive; set me up for verbal and physical abuse after the senior prom

Ranch summer workers - Sexual abuse

Who else is to come?

When I finished writing all those names and what they did to me, it just hit at that very point about all that had happened to me in just seventeen years.

Well, as I said, they did a lot of bad to me. So much so that I had just become a shell of myself, with absolutely no confidence, no self-esteem, no love, no caring anymore, numb, along with so many other emotions.

So going back to what Cathy said in the car that I was a fighter, I resigned myself to just keep doing that. And what helped me was my dream and goal to get to Munich and dive in the Olympic pool. Perhaps that would make me a man, and finally make Robert proud—even with him being so far from me.

With regards to the verse speaking about God as my helper, I quickly concluded that this was not the case, but it seemed to be just the opposite. In that moment, I broke down and started screaming at Him, if He even existed, as to where He was when all of this brutality was unfolding. Was I truly cursed by Him?

That's how I ended my journal entry on that day. I closed the journal, tucking that all away with it.

One day at a school assembly, an Army recruiter was there and gave a presentation about joining the U.S. Armed Forces.

He a was in a nice-looking uniform with many decorations. He looked like a true soldier. I listened with great interest as he spoke about not just being a soldier, but also something along the lines of, "The world is at Your feet and it's Yours to see. It will change Your life. And as a bonus with joining, you would be guaranteed Your first station of duty within the United States, and after that tour's completion, you would be able to choose another destination of Your liking." He also said that one would be free to choose the field of interest or study that one wanted to.

My first thought was, *Okay, I'm listening*, and I understand that I must have an initial tour of duty within the United States, but without telling him, my choice had already been made for my second assignment—Germany. I did briefly contemplate about the "I will be Your helper" verse in Hebrews 13. Could this be God wanting to help me? I thought to myself, *we will see.*

He continued talking about the benefits of being in the Army. At that time, the U. S. Army had just started a new recruiting program called "Be all you can be" and I said to myself, *Chase, to be all you can be would be opening up a completely new world for you, allowing you to escape from all of what you had gone through up until now.* It sounded not only hopeful but also good.

After the conclusion of his presentation, he said he would stay and be open to take any questions. I waited for a while until he was alone.

I approached him, and we started talking. I begin asking him questions about different occupations (which, he told me, are "military occupation specialties (MOS's)." I also inquired about places that I would potentially like to serve at. He presented to me a brochure that showed all of the MOS's that one could work in, along with the different locations that matched each of those occupation specialties.

We spoke for quite a while. I told him that after looking at the brochures and documents, I was very interested in continuing on with these talks, that I was very interested in joining the U. S. Armed Forces.

I thought to myself that at this point in my life, it appeared that a door was opening for me, but ultimately, I guess in looking at my inner motives, this was the perfect opportunity to just flee.

I told the recruiter that I would take the material with me for a closer look. He gave me his business card and told me to call him at any time if I had questions of him.

After I got home from school, I put my things away and then, instead of doing my homework, I headed out for a walk to the tree and took the brochures and material with me. I looked at them with great interest and after looking through all of them, in that moment I decided that I wanted to join the U.S. Armed Forces, and perhaps as the recruiter said, "be all I can be."

I was excited, I was pumped. I was on another mission.

I called him the next day and expressed my interest. We scheduled an appointment for him to come and meet me after school the next day. I was so excited about that. When we did meet, he told me more about the U.S. Armed Forces and all of the advantages, and of course the potential risks that were involved, such as combat duty. As he said that, I thought to myself that combat has been a big part of my life. And also, I thought back to that verse, *what can man do to me?*

I told him that I wanted to study stenography, and that I had decided that my first place of duty after that would be Fort Carson Colorado. I had actually chosen Fort Carson the day before in taking a map of the United States Army bases in front of me on my desk, closing my eyes, and just saying a quick thought or prayer (to what or whoever was listening) and let my finger fall where it may. And Fort Carson it was.

The recruiter said that this would be possible. He then informed me that the necessary paperwork must be filled in and completed. He informed me that, as I was under eighteen years old, I required the consent of my parents. We completed the paperwork together. He gave me a copy and took the original to be processed at the recruitment station.

A few days later, he contacted me and said that the paperwork was completed and that he would bring it by to my parents' house, as he needed to speak with them and explain the process, and then obtain their consent.

With the hopes that they were in a receiving mode, I told my parents that evening what I had decided to do and that an Army recruiter would be coming by in a few days to speak and also to obtain their signature of approval of the consent for me to join the Army when I turned eighteen, which was just about one-and-a-half months away. My mother commented to get him here and the documents would be signed, and then something to the affect that "you'll be gone."

These were very stinging words to hear, but I did not let it bother me because I knew those signatures were my ticket out of there—out of their lives and not be a burden to them any longer. I could not wait until the recruiter came and got that part of the process completed.

He did come two days later. He was explaining the process, but in midsentence, he was interrupted by my mother. She told him to give them the paperwork and they would sign it to get it over. The recruiter had a puzzled look on his face and looked at me. I nodded for him to do as they asked.

He set the paperwork in front of them and I cannot, to this day, ever remember people signing their names so quickly to a document without even reviewing it. I was a bit shocked. After they signed, a further blow came to me when, without even saying a word, they got up from the table and left the room. That reminded me of that courtroom scene seven-plus years ago when the same thing happened. It triggered me greatly, but

THE HOLLOW MASK

I dared not show this to the recruiter. I put on another mask and thought to myself, *you will soon be leaving and that you most likely would not see them ever again.* That was how I saw it at the time.

I began busying myself reading all I could find about the Army and its history, traditions, and what it could offer. I was aware of the risks that would be involved in becoming a soldier; in the event of a war, I could be called into battle. I did not think much about that at all, as what was most important to me at that particular point was getting away, going to a new place, and hopefully starting again, this time with more success.

After graduating from high school (with honors), I knew I only had three weeks before I would be gone. For me, those three weeks could not go by fast enough. I spent as much time as I could staying out of the way of my parents, mostly at the swimming pool practicing springboard and tower diving, and also at the tree, where I had scratched out the "IWDH," and replaced it with "GB4EVR" (goodbye forever). That was my mindset.

The time did indeed go by quickly, and on my eighteenth birthday, which was not really celebrated in any way other than a quick "Happy birthday," followed up with "You will soon be gone." Those words did not bother me this time as I was just looking forward to getting out of that house.

On the day that I left my parents' home, there was not even much of the goodbye or "We hope you'll do well," but simply a mere wave of the hand, more with the back of the hand, a gesture for me to just go away. I steeled myself, turned around, and got into the vehicle that came to pick me up. When the car drove off, this time, I did not look back at them.

Induction went fairly well. I was processed and then issued with uniforms and all that goes with it, including shaving my hair completely bald!

What followed was the formal part of the induction, which consisted of taking an oath as a soldier, then becoming a Government Issue, or G. I., which in my research, originally stood for "galvanized iron," the main material used to make metal iron items such as buckets, helmets, and such.

Just before the oath was administered, they informed us that we were about to become government issues, which, according to them, meant we in effect became property of the U. S. government. That again reminded me of the courtroom scene so many years ago, being told that, in effect, I had become, in my mind, property of the state.

This time, I wanted to get it right, really having no desire to please anyone else, whether my parents or my foster parents; no, this time it was for me.

They read the oath, and with my right hand raised, I repeated those words:

"I do solemnly swear that I will support and defend the Constitution of the United States against all enemies, foreign and domestic; that I will bear true faith and allegiance to the same; and that I will obey the orders of the President of the

United States and the orders of the officers appointed over me, according to regulations and the Uniform Code of Military Justice. So help me God."

With that, and maybe sounding a bit weird, I had new owners, and perhaps, this time around, I would fare much better.

Basic training lasted eight weeks, the time just flying by. From the day of arrival, right after getting off the bus, and until completion of basic training, we had a drill sergeant that was very "in Your face." His face would be literally 1 inch from mine and as he screamed at the top of his voice. Words such as, "I'll make a man and soldier out of you if it the last thing I do!" His usage of the word "man" took me back to my foster father.

What I learned and what was important to know is that just as quickly as he started yelling, he could also turn it off just as quickly. As we had been told in indoctrination, these tactics were used by drill sergeants to instill respect, aggression, and help soldiers cope with combat stress. With all of that I was okay, but respect was, for me, something that had to be earned.

We were constantly assessed for our ability to handle stress, little sleep, standing outside for long periods in pouring rain, being subjected to a lot of insults, and yes, even the remarks about one's appearance or behavior. As I wrote earlier, I had a small frame and was not the most masculine of sorts. I put on my "try and be tough" mask and somehow saw it through. As I also had been forewarned, the drill sergeants were also tasked with singling out perceived undesirables and making things tougher for them.

They did this with me, but I said to myself that I am not going to cave in this time. I am not going to be passive; I am going to get through this ordeal. It was extremely hard for me, but I knew that I could do it.

With all of the forced pushups I was forced to perform, all of the pull-ups, sit-ups, and such, I would sometimes do twice or three times more than were required, because I had my goal, my dream, engraved in the forefront of my mind, the Munich Olympia pool. So I was, at any cost, not going to fail this time around.

I am not really a firearms weapons advocate or supporter. But to my great surprise, and to that of the other soldiers and most notably, my drill sergeant, I managed to achieve an expert status in both the M16 rifle for marksmanship and tossing of the hand grenade. I was proud of myself. This time around, I thought to myself, *I will show all of you!* And in my mind, I did just that then.

At the conclusion of basic training, the drill sergeant who had so taunted and tormented me and spent so much time berating me for what he thought I had been doing so wrong, came up to me after the graduation ceremony and told me that, from my arrival there, he thought I would fail miserably.

He conceded that he was wrong and that I proved myself to keep my cool under pressure and that my level of self-discipline had surprised him and the leadership. He then, in his own way, wanted to apologize for being so hard on me. He wanted to continue, and I asked for permission to speak. He said yes, and I looked at him squarely in his eyes, and said, "Drill Sergeant, you did well, and you have my respect." In the first moment, he really did not know how to react, and without saying anything, he shook my hand, tilted his drill sergeant hat, winked, smiled, and walked away. That blew me away.

After basic training, it was off to Advanced Individual Training (AIT). This was an eighteen-week training in the field of stenography. I loved every minute of my time there. I was, for the most part, accepted and there were not very much cajoling or bad things said about me. I poured myself into my studies and really enjoyed learning shorthand. The time just shot by. A few days before graduation, I was called into the dean's office. I was surprised to learn that I had finished first in my class. That floored me, because there were some very qualified and experienced students in my class. I was elated!

With this news came the offer for the student finishing at the top of the class: to forego their original station and instead be assigned to Washington, D. C. After almost picking myself off the floor with the news of finishing at the top of my class, something inside me told me to accept this offer and go to Washington. As I stated earlier with regards to high school, my favorite subjects were U. S. government and politics. With that, I accepted and begin looking forward to moving there.

On the first day of my assignment in Washington, D. C., I decide to walk from the barracks to the Pentagon, which was not a long distance. It was a beautiful day, and I thought the fresh air would do me good and hopefully calm me down a bit.

I was looking forward to starting my new job and my mind was racing thinking about the potential new adventures that might await me, especially the thought of moving to Germany one day.

I was deep in those thoughts when, suddenly, a black limousine pulled up beside me. I noticed that it had a couple of cars behind it. I became terrified as to what might happen. The front car passenger door opened, and out stepped a soldier dressed in a nice green uniform. He ordered me to get in the back of the car. My first thought was to flee, but for some reason, I did that and found myself in the back of that car with another soldier sitting there, who looked at me and, in a very loud and commanding voice, told me, "Private, you have exactly 11 minutes to get my shoes shined, and they had better be so shiny that I can see myself in them."

His shoes were on the floorboard and there was a shoe shining kit next to them. I just picked up both and started shining as fast and as hard as I could. The man was on the car phone and appeared to be very busy and stressed. I remember glancing up at him, and on his shoulders were four stars. We had learned about military ranks in basic training and also learned that four stars were the highest rank, so I immediately knew that this man was someone very important, but I never dreamed that I would have anything to do with such high-ranking soldiers.

I continued with the shining, and for what seemed like each minute that had passed, I was yelled at that there were just a few minutes left and that I had better hurry up and get the task done. I was not at all paying attention to where we were headed in such a hurry. After finishing shining his shoes and he was putting them on, I looked out the window and saw that we were driving through a tall, opened gate. As the car entered, there appeared the White House. I remember studying about it throughout school and always wanted to visit there, as this was the place where so many presidents lived and work, and so many important events happened here, which always had fascinated me during my studies. But never in my wildest dreams did I expect to see it for the first time in this way.

As the vehicle came to a stop at the portico, the general turned to me and said, "This is where you get out." I did and immediately, several secret service agents approached me. The agents escorted me by the arm to the same gate we had entered. As we got to the gate, I told them that I needed to get to the Pentagon to work and that I would be late. The agent pointed to a parked car and told me that it would take me to the Pentagon.

My mind was reeling as I entered the car and thinking, *wow, you made it to the White House and what a treat*, albeit under these circumstances, but my mind was also wondering what would happen when I arrived late for my first day of work.

The driver sensed my nervousness and told me that I had nothing to worry about, that things had been taken care of. When we arrived at the Pentagon, the driver instructed me to report to the main entrance front desk. I did that and from there, I was escorted to my new place of work. I was excited, nervous, but also still in a bit of shock from what had just happened that morning.

I was greeted in my new office, which turned out to be the entrance and reception area. I was shown my workplace, where the walls were all wood paneled and very thick, dark blue curtains in the windows. I was shown a very beautiful and large desk, a computer table, and two long telephones on the desk with a lot of buttons. I quickly noted that almost all of those buttons were blinking. And I sat down at my desk and remembered thinking, *well, this is a far cry from where I had come from, and that just this time maybe, things would start looking up.*

As I was sitting there with my mind thinking about how this will all work out, the door to the office opened and a voice called out, "Stand up and at attention, soldier!"

I did that very quickly. As I stood there, a line of people entered the suite and at the end was a man with four stars on his shoulders. My jaw literally dropped—it was the general from the car, whose shoes I had so fervently and quickly polished. I just wanted to crawl under my desk. He appeared very busy, but he did look at me. He then told the others with him to proceed into his office, leaving him and me alone. I was thinking that I would receive yet another admonishment, and immediately braced for it to come.

To my great surprise, he offered me his hand and thanked me for the great job I had done with his shoes and that his meeting with the president had gone very well. What, the president of the United States? I stood there frozen in place, not really knowing what to say; it all seemed so surreal. And then he, who turned out to be the chief of staff of the United States Army, told me, "Well done, soldier, you did a great job under much pressure and little time." He patted me on the back and told me once again that my task was well performed, that he was proud of me, and then said, "Welcome to the Pentagon and to my team." He told me that I would be working for him. He turned and went into his office.

I could not even begin to believe or take in what just had happened. I looked at my right hand and thought, *wow, the hand that I had just shaken had shaken the hand of the president.*

My job in his office was so much fun and very rewarding. As the chief's stenographer, he would dictate texts regularly, ask me to read portions of the texts back, finish up, and then return to my desk and convert his dictation into a document. I came to enjoy spending time with him as he always asked me each day as to how I was doing and that he was very satisfied and happy with my work. Those positive words were hard for me to accept at first, but I started to learn and accept that maybe he just did mean what he said. I was basically happy and somewhat content for the first time since I had won first prize in cliff diving at the YMCA Summer Camp, now some eight years behind me.

It made me feel good. It made me feel wanted.

One day, the thought occurred to me that I still had that Bible in my backpack. As I was on my lunch break in the courtyard, I took it out of the backpack and opened it. One day as I was eating and reading, the chief was in the courtyard having lunch with a group of people. He saw me sitting alone and at some point, came over to me. He noticed that I was reading my Bible. He told me that He also should do more of that and then asked me if I could show him what I was reading. He looked at it, said something like "That is very true" and left without comment. Sometime later, after I had forgotten about meeting him, there was a package on my desk, and inside, was a plaque with this verse engraved on it, along with two open hands.

"See, I will not forget you for I have carved Your name on the palms of my hands." (Isaiah 49:16)

On the reverse side of the plaque was a "Thank you" along with his signature.

I thought, *wow, how could he have ever remembered that?* I was very happy and when he came into my office later that day. I stood up to thank him. He took my hand and told me that this verse showed him many times who he was in God and that the Lord had helped him so many times in his long career. I was deeply moved by this, of another person telling me they were a believer. Hence, this verse is on the dedication page of this book.

I poured myself into my work, looking forward to it every day. I traveled extensively with the chief and saw so many places and learning many new things. I met people who held very important and critical jobs and tried to learn from them as much as possible—from the Pentagon, the State Department, the White House, state governments, as well as many foreign ones. Sadly, Germany was not one of them. I was ill when the chief traveled there. I thought to myself that my time has not come, but it would.

One of the most exciting times of my tour of duty there was when the only remaining five star general, General of the Army Omar Bradley, came to Washington, D.C. He was quite old and in a wheelchair. He had a suite of two offices for when he was in town. I was tasked with ensuring that he had everything he needed and was made as comfortable as possible.

I had studied about his illustrious career in the Army during World War II and had written reports about him in my world history class. His second wife traveled with him. She and I got along very well, even with her reported temper. I witnessed that from her with many others, but never with me. I was fascinated by the general then, and now here I was tasked with taking care of him and his wife.

He visited several times while I was there, and really, he wanted nothing more than to have someone sit with him and tell stories about the war. His wife sat with us at times, but she was mostly engaged with other activities. I hung on every word he told me. I could not help thinking of the people he had direct contact with—Eisenhower, Truman, Patton, Marshall, MacArthur, Pershing, as well as many other leaders from around the world. He was an absolutely fascinating man, and I would sit there engrossed in stories that had actually happened.

My mind tried to put into pictures what he was telling me. I cherished those times. To me, he had certainly earned and lived up to his title, "The GI's General."

Things were going very well. I was accepted at work, at the barracks, and from most other people. To my surprise, here was not taunting, no name calling, no abuse in any form. I thought that finally my time had come to leave all of that behind me.

One of the humorous parts of my job, well for me anyway, was when the weekly run came to destroy no-longer needed classified documents. I was given a very high security clearance, and it was my job to ensure that all the documents were accounted for being placed in the secured wagon. Each week, two military policemen came to the office and escorted me and the wagon on each side. We would roll it through the corridor until we came to an elevator. That elevator took us down to a large room with no windows. There was a conveyor belt rolling upwards, and we would place the documents on the conveyor belt and they were taken up and landed in a large container.

The machine was already running, and I remember the first time we made this run, I was allowed to stay and see what happened to all those documents. Were they shredded, incinerated or water-pulped? To my surprise, the machine turned those sensitive documents into nothing other than toilet paper, churning them out in commercial-size toilet paper rolls. I chuckled at the time, and then, excuse the vulgarity, I said, "Shit happens."

On one foreign trip to England with the chief, he had meetings scheduled with high-ranking officials, including a senior-ranking government diplomat. I usually attended the meetings to take notes and transcribe them for the record. I thoroughly enjoyed being a part of what I always called "high stakes" meetings, those that would at times take place in Cuban-cigar-smoked rooms with very expensive brandy. I felt really important being there, like I had finally made it. Was this the answer to my question of "who am I?"

During one of the breaks, the British diplomat approached me and asked me what my name was. As he shook my hand, I told him my name. He asked me if I was enjoying England and I said that from what I had so far seen, I liked it. It was basic small talk.

He asked me what I was doing later in the afternoon. I said that that the chief would be occupied, leaving me with the rest of the day free. He said the same for himself and offered to pick me up and show me around London. I thought that was a very nice gesture of him and was looking forward to it. After the conclusion of the meeting, I went back to our hotel, got a quick nap, showered, and got ready. His driver called my room and I went downstairs and got in the car. It was a great afternoon as we took in many sites of this great city. My thought was that it was very nice and kind of him to do this for me.

After touring, he asked me if I wanted to join him for dinner at his diplomatic residence. Without much thought, I said yes. We drove to a fantastic place. We had a wonderful meal in a large dining room with an open fireplace. It was very relaxing for me. He was very engaging and asked me questions about my past. With that, and because of lack of trust, I immediately put on my confabulation mask. I told him that I had a wonderful childhood and upbringing. I was lying, but I could not afford to expose the truth again and again be betrayed.

We talked for a very long time, enjoying drinks. The time seemed to fly by. The conversation turned a bit more personal as he probed me about having a girlfriend, to which I honestly answered I did not. He then told me that he was married with three children, but that his very busy work schedule kept him away from his family most of the time, and that family life just did not seem to satisfy him. My first thought was, *if that were the case, then what I am doing here with him this evening when he said he had no plans and nowhere to be.* That put me on edge. But in my mind, I reasoned that he was not in a good place personally and it seemed to me that he was being honest and sincere. I told him that I was sorry to hear this.

It was late, but we had another drink served and then he asked the staff to leave. I said something to the affect that I thought I should be getting back to the hotel as we had a busy day planned ahead. He got up from his place at the table and came over to me and told me that tomorrow will come and go, but that we only really have right now and should "take advantage" of the time. Those words made me very nervous. I told him that I would like to return back to the hotel.

I got up from my chair and we walked towards the cloak room. When we entered there, I was looking for my coat and my back was turned against him. All of a sudden, he grabbed me from behind, taking both of my hands into his hand along with his other around the back of my neck so that I could not move. What happened next is more than I dare to put into words, but it was horrible. While the brutal sexual attack was occurring, my mind returned back to that that jail cell some ten years earlier. I remember thinking, *what is happening here, and why again now?* Things were going so well.

When it was over, I found myself on the cloak room floor. He towered over me and looked down on me and told me that if I ever told anyone about this, he would personally see to it that I would be destroyed, both professionally and personally. Then he did something that just floored me. He took out his wallet, took some bills out, and hurled them at me. He told me to find my own way back to the hotel. I got myself dressed and quickly got out of there.

I was able to hail a taxi and return back to the hotel, shattered and battered. When I got back to my room, I again showered for what seemed like an eternity, in a vain attempt to remove the filth of what just happened. Here it was, history repeating itself. I ask myself to this date why I did not scream and kept it quiet? He was a very important man, and his threats terrified me. In that moment, I hated him and myself so much.

I managed to crawl into bed, those threatening words going through my mind. I knew full well that I could not tell anyone about what had happened, because I would most likely not be believed. I tried as best as I could to shut the whole incident off my mind. At some point, I fell asleep, exhausted, and feeling so alone once again. I just kept asking, *why? Why is this happening again? What signals had I been sending? Just what is wrong with me?* There was no one there to help me, or maybe at this point I was beyond help.

The next morning, I awoke with so many thoughts going through my mind. I knew I would see him again in meetings planned for that day. I had to steel myself to get through it all. The chief asked me at some point if I was doing okay. I lied to him by saying that I had a bad headache and that it would pass.

When the diplomat entered the meeting room a bit later, chills were running through me. During the entire time he was there, he acted as though I was not even in the room. I do not recall him looking at me or acknowledging me. I wanted to scream at the top of my lungs about what he had done to me, but I just could not. The stakes were too high. It was very hard. That was one meeting that I was very happy to have behind me.

As we were flying back to Washington, all my mind was telling me that the plane was flying in the wrong direction. For whatever reason, it would have been much better flying east-bound in the direction of Germany. That was my goal, my mission, and my fighting spirit (*Kampfgeist*) knew that I would make it there someday. I decided to stay quiet.

After returning to Washington, I tried my best to pretend that the incident in England was behind me, that it did not happen. I was compartmentalizing. It was easier for me to process.

The next day at work, I had a lot to accomplish and the task list was growing. I liked that because I knew it would keep me busy. It would keep my mind off of so many other things, including the past.

A week or so later, I received a call mid-morning from a fellow soldier and friend of mine, Lisa. We had become friends at advanced training and we were both selected to be assigned in Washington because of our high standing in the class. She asked me if I would join her for lunch in the courtyard. I said yes and we met at noon.

She was already there when I arrived and she seemed very upset. I asked her what was wrong. After a bit of probing, she told me that she was pregnant. I knew she had a boyfriend and that he was married, with children, and more senior in rank to her, an officer at that. She was falling apart in front of me and was very worried as to what could happen if this all came out into the open, especially with fraternization within the ranks.

I tried to calm her down as best as I could. I asked her if there was something I could do for her. She said yes, and then told me that she was strongly considering aborting the child, but that she could not do that on her own. She needed the father's consent. She told me that there was no way she would tell her boyfriend about this.

I really was not sure what my stance on abortion was at the time, but I suggested she carefully think this over and ultimately inform her boyfriend. If she did not want to tell her boyfriend, she should seek counseling before making this irreversible decision.

I told her that I had to return to work and that we could meet again after my shift was completed. I felt bad leaving her in her condition. My thoughts were with her during the rest of the afternoon.

We did meet after work. She asked me if we could walk along the Potomac River, to which I said yes. It had become a favorite jogging place of mine. We walked for a long time, mostly in silence, and then she asked me if we could go to the Lincoln Memorial.

I said yes and we proceeded to go there. When we arrived, she asked me if we could sit on the stairs. We did and after what seemed like a long time of silence, she turned to me and took my hand into hers. Her next words took me completely by surprise.

She told me that she had decided to abort the child and that she had made an appointment at an abortion clinic to have the procedure done the following week in Washington. I asked her if she had spoken to her boyfriend about this. She said no and would and could not do this.

I probed as to how she wanted to go through this procedure without him knowing. She began begging me if I would agree to say that I was the father and that I would give my consent to the abortion. As I was totally unprepared for such a question, I was completely bowled over.

I remember saying to myself that this is something that I did not want to do, knowing internally that I did think that an abortion was not the answer, in addition to it all being a lie. I also knew that an innocent life would be taken, and to me, it would be murder.

At the same time, I knew what could happen to her and her boyfriend and what the harsh punishment could be regarding fraternization and her getting pregnant. It could ruin both of their careers and reputations, not to mention my own.

Before I could begin to give her my answer, she literally broke down there, on those historical monument stairs, and begin begging me with even greater intensity, telling me that I am the only person she could turn to and completely trust. I thought once again, *Here comes another trust issue.*

I was so torn as to what to do. I also had to think of the consequences that I could face if this procedure went through and came out into the open. At that time, with the military laws in place, that could make me an accessory to a Uniformed Code of Military Justice (UCMJ) offense.

Still reeling from the events in England, and being in an almost unbearable emotional state myself, I realized that she did not, as she usually would have, ask me how the trip went and how I was doing. Under the circumstances, though, I concluded that it was better that she did not, and so I just kept myself focused on the issue at hand—her predicament.

I know that it was her choice to be in a relationship with her boyfriend and when she told me about it, I remember commenting that this could wind up not ending well.

So, part of me concluded that she knew the rules and that she had been warned about what the potential consequences could be for their actions. I remember saying to myself that I did not cause this problem and that this is something that she would have to deal with, foremost telling him that she was pregnant.

I asked her just how important this relationship was to her, considering that he was married with children and again telling her about the serious potential consequences of this whole thing.

She said that she loved him with all of her heart and would do anything to not lose him, including an abortion. She proceeded to plead with me for what seemed like an eternity. I was physically and mentally worn out, just exhausted, and did not know if I would even have the strength myself to go through with this, if I did make the decision to do so.

As I continued to try and process what was going on, she told me that she knew things about me that could prove to be very detrimental, and that I, too, could face serious punishment if this ever was revealed. That comment caught me totally off guard. Was she attempting to blackmail me and reveal those very private things we shared as friends (is that what friends do?) if I did not do what she wanted me to? She knew so much as I had opened up to her over time (she was the first). It frightened me a lot. The possibilities of what could happen were racing through my mind.

This made me question whether she had my best interests at hand, and with that, if she was even a true friend. Up to this point in my life, I had never really had one, so I did not know what it really was to have that kind of friend.

She continued to press for me for an answer. I was so weak and at some point, I conceded and told her yes, even knowing that I should not take part in this. But with her veiled attempt at blackmail, I could forget about Germany and all the plans I had made so long ago.

One might ask whether I had thought about turning the tables on her and threatened to expose her and her boyfriend? The answer should be a resounding yes, but after having so many tables turned on me, I just could not do this to someone else, especially someone I considered a friend. Was this incorrect thinking? Read on.

As we returned back to the barracks, walking again mostly in complete silence, so much was running through my mind. It was so difficult thinking that this might be a reprehensible and wicked thing that I was about to take part in.

We said good night and I went back to my room, somehow thinking about what would God think of this and how He would see this. I remember learning in Sunday school that the sixth commandment forbids direct and intentional killing as gravely sinful. I remember the Sunday school teacher telling us that the murderer, or those who participate and cooperate voluntarily in murder commit, in his words at the time, "an abominable, wicked, and depraved act."

That night, I did not sleep at all.

At work the next day, I tried to distract myself and not think about what was ahead of me. The days leading up to the appointment at the abortion clinic seemed to race by, and before I knew it, that day came. She had borrowed a car from a friend, and I had managed to get the permission to take the day off from work. She asked me if I would drive, and what was a 20-minute drive seemed to take forever. My mind was reeling in agony as to what I was about to take part in, most critically the huge lie I was about to tell. This would violate the ninth commandment on do not lie.

We arrived at the clinic and before getting out of the car, I asked her again if she was certain she really wanted to go through with this. She said yes, and without even asking me if I wanted this, she added, "Come on, let's get this over with."

"Let's get this over with"? I questioned. It was clear to me that she had convinced herself that "this" had nothing to do with the human life within her.

I did get out of the car and entered the clinic. It struck me as a very cold and very sterile environment, not a place where life is celebrated. After reporting to the front desk, we were given what seemed like a stack of paperwork and led to a treatment room. Both of us sat in complete silence as we read the documents that they had given us. There was a statement at the end of each document that said not to sign the documents without having the attending physician and a member of the clinic staff being present as witnesses.

After waiting for a while, the physician and a staff member entered the room and sat down opposite us. The line of question was along the lines if this is really what we wanted to do and if I, as the father, were willing to grant my permission to allow the procedure to take place.

Me, the father? I just wanted to get up, shout at the top of my lungs that I was not the father, and get out of there. But the notion of being blackmailed and at that point in my mind, losing it all, my hopes and dreams, persuaded me otherwise.

As you are reading this and perhaps making Your own conclusions and judgments, I will share that I allowed myself to be put under such immense pressure. It did not help that I had an overwhelming need to please other people at almost any cost. Deep down, I knew that I should not be taking part in this, but I did. Time will be the judge of my action.

But I caved in, and when the doctor placed the document in front of me to sign, I knew that I was signing what was, in my mind, a death sentence, based on great deception and terrible lying. As I wrote out each letter of my signature, my thought was had I completely lost all of my moral compass, or was one even there to begin with? I closed my eyes and finished signing the document.

I was then instructed to go to the waiting room while the procedure was being done. As I was getting ready to go there, I looked at Lisa. It was clear her mind was completely somewhere else. As they led me out of the room, I tried to get her attention, but it seemed, to her, I was not even there. I felt completely hollow and sat completely numb in the waiting room, really with not much going through my mind. I just did not have the capacity to think anymore.

When the staff member came to the waiting room, I knew the procedure was over and that an innocent life had just been taken; a life was over before it even really begun, and I found myself breaking down in great sorrow and tears. What had I just taken part in? How could I have gone through with this?

The staff member sat down next to me and told me that she, too, after each procedure, asked herself how she could continue to take part in such atrocities, at which point I just did not want to listen to anything else, and so I motioned to her with my hand to stop and asked about how Lisa was doing. The staff member told me that the procedure was successful and that Lisa would be released a bit later in the day. My mind was racing as to what that child would be missing out on, and that this child did not even have a chance or decision in the matter.

When Lisa entered the waiting room, I stood up and stepped towards her. I was shocked to see a smile on her face. I wanted to hug her and tell her how sorry I was, but she stepped back and simply said, "It's over. Let's go." I was so taken aback by that very cold response.

On the way back to the barracks, she turned the radio on to a rock music station and it was very loud. I could hardly hear myself think. After a bit, I reached over and turned the radio down. I then looked over at her, and she still had that very awful smile on her face. That really bothered me and I could not contain my silence any longer.

As we pulled into the barracks parking space, I decided to ask why she was smiling and acting as though nothing happened. Her response flattened me. She opened the door, and before getting out of the car, she did not even thank me but turned to me and said, "It's gone and I am happy about that. You did Your part, so just please keep Your mouth shut." She then slammed the door and walked away. I could only try to imagine what an arrogant look she must have had on her face.

But what she left behind was not a nineteen-year-old man but a very insecure, unwanted, scorned, and once again, rejected boy. *What had just happened?* I asked myself.

Another betrayal, another case of just being used? After that, we really did not see each other again. When we did cross paths, at times with her boyfriend, she would only nod her head and keep walking. We never spoke again about what happened. And then we just lost touch with each other.

I was deeply hurt. I was confused, and I was angrier about this than anything that had happened in my life to date. I was set up once again, and this time, the price was just too high for me—an innocent baby had been murdered. And with that, I took on even more guilt and shame. I realized in that moment that even more of me had died inside. How could I have let this happened?

And yet again, even with all of the betrayal on her part, I chose to forgive her but not myself. I just hated myself more and more. I was the abominable, wicked, and depraved one.

The events that took place in England and with Lisa started to take a huge toll on me. I was exhausted, worn out, and just feeling hollow. I poured myself more and more into my work. It became an obsession with me to work even harder and try to forget the past two events, if that were even possible.

I also did a lot of sports, including jogging, weightlifting, and springboard diving, all of which would take my mind off things, albeit temporarily. But I knew something was off, and I knew things must change, but the question I kept asking myself was would it be for the better or worse?

I had some very memorable times in Washington. Working for the chief and other senior officials at the Pentagon, I was exposed to a world that was so fascinating and very rewarding. There was structure and discipline, along with great responsibility. At the same time, I was in awe of the fact that I worked at the seat of government, with very high-ranking people who made very critical decisions that affected so many.

My superiors would always take the time to ask how I was doing or tell me that I did a good job, and they made me feel welcomed. I had never really experienced that until then. I was able to see so much and travel to many places that I never dreamed of.

And attending so many functions in Washington, at the Pentagon, the State Department, or at the White House (and these times I actually entered—not like the shoe shining incident), along with witnessing history in so many critical and important meetings, or with high-ranking foreign guests, it was just such a thrill. I was very thankful for the opportunities given to me. I felt needed, trusted, and valued. All of these helped build my self-esteem and self-worth. These are wonderful memories that I will treasure and not forget.

Even so, I continued to put on so many different masks. I could not allow myself to open up to anyone. There was just too much pain and absolute sadness. I could not open up to what had happened there and other seedy places, some of which I participated in the underground of Washington with Lisa, including hard drugs, sex, excessive alcohol consumption, just to name a few. And with illegal drugs, the possibility of severe punishment and discipline, including a dishonorable discharge and potential prison time.

I was just so careless, reckless, and not thinking about any potential consequences. In doing so, a pattern of self-destructive behavior began to manifest within me. I had become a totally different person.

With all that happened in Washington, good and bad, I made the decision to move on. Perhaps it's all due to wanderlust. I did not realize at that time that there were very deep, underlying psychological problems. I will write about this later on.

I knew all too well that there were people at work who had taken such good care of me and were very kind and respectful. That made me feel accepted and wanted. But at that time in the

Army, there was no real open door to receive counseling and therapy. It was frowned upon back then, so I tried to "bandage" those deep psychological wounds with fleeing, before I could be sent away and rejected yet again.

I arranged for an appointment at the Pentagon personnel department to inquire about a transfer. I told the staff worker that I would like to be reassigned. Before I could tell him that I would like to consider an assignment in Europe, specifically Germany, he was already typing on his computer—his thoughts seemed to be a million miles away. I was about getting ready to ask if he had even heard my question, he looked at me and said that a position with my MOS had just become available that morning. I asked where and he answered, "Munich, Germany." His words floored me. I could not believe what I was hearing. Before even accepting the offer, I remember saying to myself, *Thank you whoever! I am not only moving to Munich, Germany, but also the home of the Olympia Park Diving Center!*

The staff worker saw that my mind was somewhere else and he asked me what was wrong, and that brought me back into reality. He informed that I had eighteen months remaining on active duty. I asked if it would be possible to reenlist in Germany, and he said that it was.

That relieved me greatly because I knew I wanted to stay in Germany, thinking I would remain a soldier. He then asked me if this assignment would be acceptable to me. I said, "Springboard diving awaits."

The look on his face was very puzzled. I knew he did not understand my answer, so I quickly apologized and said, "Yes, sir, let's make this happen."

My boss told me that he was sorry to see me depart, but that he understood that I wanted to transfer to Germany, as I had shared my dream of going there on several occasions with him. He told me about his several tours there and would tell me about how beautiful the country was. He told me that I had served exceptionally and with integrity and honor. He said that it was a pleasure to have me on his staff. Those were very kind words from him.

I continued to work for six weeks and then out processed. The chief and his staff arranged for a very nice farewell party for me, including awarding me my second Army Commendation Medal. It was very special to me, and yes, in a way, I was sad to leave, but in my mind, my goal of finally getting to Germany was now about to become reality.

The Army arranged for a flight on a Thursday. They told me that I would be flying commercial. As I was checking in for the flight, the check in attendant asked me if I was traveling alone. I said I was. She then told me they were upgrading me complimentary to a first-class seat. This was my first time flying first class. I thought to myself, *wow, I have waited all these years to get to Germany, and with the extra blessing of flying first class!* I felt so important. It was one of the first times in my life that I felt that way.

The flight was fantastic. I was able to get some sleep in and I woke up in a very happy, thankful, and excited state. We landed in Munich on Friday morning. I said to myself, *Chase, you finally made it.* As I stepped out of the terminal onto German soil, the sun had just come up. It became a very warm and beautiful day.

I was picked up at the airport and was taken to McGraw Kaserne, about three miles southeast of Munich city center. Having looked at a map, I knew the Kaserne was about a 20-minute commute to the Olympia Park. McGraw was the home of the Army and Air Force Exchange Service, the 66th Military Intelligence Group, and the University of Maryland. Later, it was host to the European Racquetball Championships, a sport I learned to play while stationed there.

After arriving, I was in processed and taken to my barracks room, and then given a tour of the facilities there. After that, the Charge of Quarters (CQ) told me that I had the weekend free, that I was report to duty on Monday morning.

I could not get my belongings unpacked fast enough, as all I wanted to do was to get to the Olympia Park and fulfill my childhood dream. After taking a quick shower, I got my backpack ready and headed to the front gate of the Kaserne.

There were German taxis waiting there. Not knowing how to get to the Olympia Park and with very limited knowledge of the German language, I got in the first taxi and told the driver where I wanted to go. I tried to do this in my best German. To my surprise, the driver said that he spoke English. Relieved to hear that, I told him I wanted to go to the Olympia Park. We got to talking and he told me that he was a driver for athletes at the 1972 Summer Olympics and that he met so many of them, including several Israeli athletes who lost their lives during the terrorist attacks. That saddened me.

As the taxi approached the Olympic village, I was awestruck by just how huge the grounds were. It certainly was much larger than what I had seen on that small TV screen nine-and-a-half years ago.

The driver told me that we would pass the Israeli athletes' dorms. As we did, the driver stopped and told me that he was there that day and witnessed some of the tragedy unfolding. It was extremely difficult for him and he began to weep uncontrollably. I felt so sorry for him and asked if there was something I could do for him. It was clear to me that this event traumatized him immensely. In that moment, it made my own traumatic events seem trivial; I was still alive.

He told me that Germany wanted the Munich Olympic Games to be the opposite of the 1936 Berlin Olympic games, nearly three decades after the Holocaust. The plan was to try and erase that symbolism of the country's Nazi past. Germany wanted this Summer Olympics to be "the cheerful games."

Sadly, that did not happen. In what became known as Black September, Palestinian extremists murdered eleven Israeli athletes and coaches, along with one German police officer. The attack was the first time that a global audience of around 900 million people witnessed an act of terrorism as it unfolded on their television sets. That event drastically changed the way the world thought about terrorism; as a soldier, it certainly changed mine.

The driver, Josef, regained his composure, and he finally drove to me to the diving arena. I told him how sorry I was for him that he had to go through all of that tragedy and sadness.

He told me something to the affect that has stayed with me to this day: "In this world, there will be many who try and disrupt our peace. They will try to threaten and intimidate us. It will get worse. But we should become more vigilant. We must not let this deter us from continuing to live our lives in peace and freedom."

Very wise words from him. In that moment, I hoped that those who were brutally killed had found their peace.

What Josef told me reminded me of John 14:27, which I learned way back then in Sunday school, when I could find no peace and did not even have any hope of finding it. Jesus said, "Peace I leave with you, my peace I give you. I do not give to you as the world gives. Do not let Your hearts be troubled and do not be afraid." I wanted that peace!

I paid the taxi bill and thanked him for sharing his story and his wise words. That was very special to me. I asked him if I could hug him, and he got out of the taxi. We shared a wonderful hug and I bade him goodbye and wished him God's blessings. He was physically moved and said that he could sure use those blessings. To me, and it is a sad thing to say, they were words (God's blessings) I had previously used to just finish a conversation and move on. Perhaps with Josef, this time I meant them.

He wished me a great time with diving and taught me one of my first German idioms, *"mach kein Hals-und Beinbruch."* He told me that in old German, it meant "Don't break Your neck and bones." I thought this was a bit strange (considering how dangerous diving can be). I told him that in English, we would say, "Good luck, and don't break any bones." We got a good laugh out of this all. Later when I looked up that idiom, I read that the phrase indeed means good luck, and it could have possibly also been derived from the Hebrew, *"hatzlakha u-brakha,"* meaning "success and blessing." To me, the second sounded better than the first! I went on to study and learn many German idioms and found them fascinating. I use many of them to this date.

As I got out of the taxi, my heart was beating so quickly. I had to force myself to stop and take several deep breaths to calm myself down.

I had finally made it here. I found myself standing outside the entrance to the Munich Olympiad swimming and diving arena. In that moment, it seemed that all else in my life had been forgotten, as though it all had been from my memory. This was a mission long in the making, and now here I was -. finally accomplishing this mission. I pinched myself to know for sure that this was really happening!

I then entered the arena and paid for my entrance ticket. I went through the turnstile gate and, for the first time, I saw it live, the pool and the boards and towers. My mind returned to watching the competition here back in 1972.

I went to the locker room, changed into my swimsuit, walked into the large hall, and then by the Olympic swimming pool where Mark Spitz had won seven gold medals. I just stood there and imagined the excitement of it all, but at the same time, the great tragedy and sadness that overshadowed those events.

And then, finally, I approached the diving pool.

My mind was reeling about so many great events that happened here. Diving greats such as Vladimir Vasin from the Soviet Union won the gold medal on the 3-meter springboard. Klaus Dibiasi from Italy won the gold medal on the 10-meter platform. I recalled American divers Craig Howard Lincoln and Richard Anthony Rydze winning bronze and silver medals, respectively. I just could not believe that I was really here.

I stood there for what seemed like an eternity just taking it all in. I watched in awe as divers lept off the 10-meter platform and others jumping from the 3-meter springboard. Men, women, and children were all having a good time.

In the left corner of the diving area, there was a group of divers practicing. I remember thinking how good they all were; I was very impressed. I watched them for a while. There were some really great divers among them.

I steeled myself to finally achieve what I had so long yearned for. I thought to myself that this is heaven on earth. One last, quick pinch convinced me that this was real.

I was shaking, nervous, and overly emotional. And I begin to warm up behind the diving area with breathing exercises, stretches and some pushups, along with several sets of jumping jacks. This all helped me get my body ready as well as calm it down.

After the warm up, I steeled myself and began to climb up that ladder to the 3-meter springboard, which, by the way, was my favorite diving board and also my specialty.

As I stood there standing on the diving board, I just savored the moment, feeling so happy that I had finally made it. And I launched my first ever dive there, one-and-half forward flip with two twists, one of my favorite dives. It went well and, after coming up and out of the water, I felt a tremendous sense of accomplishment. I was proud of myself—I made it!

I continued diving from the 3-meter springboard and was enjoying it immensely. I was very good at this, and my diving attracted the attention of quite a few onlookers, with rounds of applause coming after several of my dives. It took me back to that applause I received in winning my first diving competition at summer camp. I felt acknowledgment and adoration. It was good.

I recall saying to myself and to Robert, "See, these people acknowledge my accomplishments with words of praise, not with words and fists of hate and rage."

I noticed out of the corner of my eye that the group of divers practicing were watching me as well. After landing a particularly difficult two-and-a-half forward dive with two twists, I came up out of the water and swam over to the ladder. As I was getting out of the water, there was a man standing there. He knew that I spoke English as I was speaking with several divers and onlookers. He told me that I was a really good diver and that he was really impressed with my abilities. He wanted to know who I was, where I was from, and how I learned to dive so well.

I thanked him, shook his hand, and introduced myself. He told me his name was Michael, his nickname Michi. I answered his questions. He told me he was there diving with his teammates and that he was sent on a mission to me by the coach to find out who I was. I admit that my head was a bit swollen with pride.

Michi asked me if I wanted to join him and his teammates. I said yes and together we walked over to the group. The coach approached me and shook my hand. He started to speak in German, and I told him that I did not speak much German. Michi volunteered to translate.

The coach told me that he was very impressed with my diving ability and told me that I was a natural talent and that my body was built just right to hit those tight angles and twists. I said thank you to him. After having been body shamed for most of my life, it felt good to hear words of encouragement along those lines. I was standing there with my right foot place over my left foot to cover up the fungus on my toenail; this was something I instinctively did when I was barefoot, mostly since my toe was chosen to be part of the perfect guy in grammar school.

It turns out that the man was the coach of the German men's national diving team. I was blown away! I could not believe my good fortune. Michi was a member of the team. And so, I spent that entire weekend diving with the team. A few of us remain friends until today, including Michi. I had an absolute blast! Could it get any better than this?

Never once did any of them ever make a pejorative remark to me, nor was there any hint of abuse that occurred there. I thought that maybe my life was finally turning around for the good. I sure could use that!

Michi and I became good friends and spent a lot of time together. We had a lot in common—diving, jogging, hiking, and mountain biking. I also taught him how to play racquetball at McGraw.

He also liked history and politics. He worked for the Bavarian State Government Interior Department.

We got along very well, and he helped me so much in learning the German language. We had many wonderful meals together, discussing so many topics, especially about the world in general, as well as government, politics, and history. This was all right up my alley.

He was a very genuine, caring, warm, humorous, honest, and most humble fellow. And when he told me that he was a Christian, it did not surprise me, and my body did not automatically tense up as it did so many years ago listening to those fiery sermons about "fire and brimstone" in church.

He told me his life story and also shared his testimony on how he had come to a saving knowledge in Christ. He said that before he came to Christ, his life was, in his words, "topsy-turvy" (I admired his use of so many American idioms, and he taught me many German ones as well).

He told me that he had reached a point in his life where he knew he could not go on in what he called "his wickedness and depravity." After meeting a friend who was a Christian, that friend told him about his life as well, which was traumatic, much like mine. He started attending church and bible studies. He then gave his life to Jesus. This time, that story touched me in a different and special way.

One day, he asked me about my life. After his sharing his story with me, and hearing those about his friends who had also given their lives to Jesus, deep inside of me, I wanted to tell him, but with my history of betrayal and mistrust, I just could not bring myself to do that.

He sensed my hesitancy, that I did not really want to talk about it, but he told me that he would be there for me should I change my mind. I told him thank you. I followed that up with the statement, "I am trying to figure out who I am." He never pressed, for which I was very thankful.

I liked my job and enjoyed the work. I received a promotion while serving there. I had a very good boss. He was an up-and-coming officer in the ranks and ultimately went on to become a two-star general. He and I had a very good and solid working relationship. He was someone I looked up to, and he was, in a way, a mentor to me.

One thing he did tell me was if one had a desire to climb the ranks, it would be much easier if one were married with children.

As he continued speaking, my mind went back to what I had gone through with my own parents and foster parents, neither couple demonstrating very little love for each other, not to mention towards me.

My mind came back into the conversation as he continued to speak, and I would occasionally nod my head, feigning interest. I simply took what he said with a grain of salt. After he was finished speaking, I thanked him and told him that I would think about it. After the conversation, it did strike me as odd as to why he would even have this conversation with me. Perhaps, he wanted to see me succeed, I do not know, but his words stuck with me. We never had a conversation about this again. In time, I put it out of my mind.

Looking back, I found that an awkward situation, comparing it to today's standards. But I realize that was a different era and culture.

I immersed myself into more sports, which consisted of squash, tennis, weightlifting, diving, and jogging. These all were a means for me to "let go" for a bit, to escape, and experience some freedom.

I then took up racquetball, a sport which I really enjoyed playing during my lunch breaks. There were some really great players there, and they helped me with playing tips and strategies. I fell in love with the game.

McGraw was the host for the European Racquetball Championships for several years. Racquetball never caught on in Europe like squash did, and after leaving the service, I missed it a lot.

I had a friend who went through basic training with me also stationed at McGraw. We did not see each other often after I arrived, but one day I came back to the barracks after work. I was very tired, but I decided that what I needed was a nice long run. I changed my clothes and was getting ready to head out. For some reason, I thought of my friend Tom and decided that I wanted to ask him to join me. He lived one floor above me.

As I knocked on his door, he opened the room and we exchanged greetings. Looking over his shoulder, I noticed he had a visitor. I told him I would come back later. He said it was all right and to come in. He said he had a German friend over for a visit.

I went into his room and sitting at the table was a young woman who stood up to greet me. Tom introduced me to her as Hannah. We shook hands and said hello to each other.

I immediately noticed that her English was good, so I asked her where she learned the language. She said that she had learned it in school and now at university. Tom commented that her English was outstanding and that they had met through the local German American "Kontakt Klub" that was designed to bring Germans and Americans together, to get to know each other and learn about the different cultures.

She also told me that English was her favorite subject. She said she preferred American English as opposed to British English. I could tell by listening to her that she had a lot of practice.

She was a bit shy, but I sensed she was humble and kind. I could also sense she had a very gentle spirit to her. I thought I admired those qualities in her and I liked her.

Tom said she had brought a homemade German cheesecake with her and a pot of herbal tea. I said this was very kind of her, that the cheesecake looked great and I hoped they would have a good time enjoying it. She asked Tom if it would be okay if I joined them and he said yes. The cheesecake tasted great and the tea was perfect.

The conversation was cordial and we spoke mostly about the Kontakt Klub. Hannah commented that her dream was to visit the United States.

Tom commented that Hannah was studying to become a teacher. She said she had always wanted to do this, as both her parents were teachers as well.

I forgot about the run as the conversation continued. It was very pleasant, and time seemed to fly by. Hannah then invited us to dinner at her favorite restaurant.

I said thank you and accepted. Tom would not be able to join us but said to go ahead with dinner and wished us a good time.

I went back to my room, cleaned up, and changed into dinner clothes.

The restaurant was her favorite, the *Waldeslust* (The Happy Forrest), located in *Unterhaching*. We had a fascinating conversation and I really liked listening to her story. I found out that she was, in her words, a "believing Christian" and that she spoke a lot about her faith, trust, and how it had, after making many mistakes, changed her own life. I asked her what she meant by that and how it changed her life. She said that that she knew that when she accepted Jesus Christ as her Savior, she was born again and had the promise of eternal life.

In my mind, red alert alarms went off, and my thoughts went immediately back to Reverend Moore and his constant babbling about being born again. I also thought of Michi. I kept quiet but continued to listen with interest. I sensed that what she was telling me came from a very humble heart.

It was similar in a lot of ways to that Michi. I begin to think that maybe what they were saying made more sense to me. I was okay with all of that. But all of these people entering into my life and telling me that they had become Christians? Was someone, perhaps God, trying to send me a message?

The restaurant was great, the food excellent, and the conversation even better. I liked her and decided in my mind that I wanted to spend more time with her, initially thinking along the lines of possibly becoming good friends.

After a wonderful evening, she drove me back to the barracks. I thanked her for inviting me. I told her that if she would like to meet again, we could do that. She said yes. I accepted her offer and said I would be looking forward to it. She gave me her phone number. I shook her hand and told her that I would be in touch with her. I got out of the car and went to my barracks room and got ready for bed. My mood was good, and after such a nice evening, I found my thoughts turning to Hannah and how things might proceed from there.

I went to work the next morning. Tom came to visit me in my office and asked how things went with Hannah. I told him it went very well. He said she would make a great catch and he encouraged me to pursue her. I nodded my head and thanked him for saying that.

After work, I met Michi at the Olympiad. In the meantime, I had started giving springboard and tower diving lessons in my free time there. I really enjoyed the coaching, and it really helped me in becoming more proficient in the German language.

After a night of great diving, Michi and I went to get a drink. We spoke about our work and my studies. I told him that I wanted to immerse myself in the German language. I told him that my goal was to stay in Germany after my active-duty time was over. He told me that he would teach me.

It was hard for me in the beginning; as I saw it, German is a very exact language as opposed to English being more relaxed. It took a while for me to understand the difference between the formal and informal in German. We met regularly. Slowly, it all started coming to me. To date, I remain so thankful to him. He was a great teacher and remains a great friend to date.

For some reason, I thought often of the Bible verse in Romans 8:28: "All things work together for good to them that love God, to them who are called according to His purpose." I questioned if I actually did love Him, or better yet, did He love me, and if so, would things really work out for good?

I remembered learning this verse in Sunday school so many years ago. I was amazed to see how this and other verses managed to stick in my memory. I had a great head knowledge of the Bible, and read it often. I started to question if God actually have a plan for me?

Hannah was also on my mind. I had good memories of our initial meeting and our dinner together. And I thought that I would like to become friends with her and take her up on her offer and spend time together and learn about the culture and the area here.

I called her a few days later and asked her how she was doing and if we could meet again. She said yes and we decided to meet on the following Saturday morning. We had a great day together as she showed me around Munich. She knew so much about the German (and Bavarian) cultures, as well as with the surrounding area.

Up until then, she did not ask me much along the lines of my personal life, but the conversation eventually turned to this. She asked me how my childhood was.

My body immediately tensed and I had to pause to think about how I would answer that question. I know she told me she had great parents, a very wonderful childhood, which was full of very good and fond memories, all of which I had dreamed of for so many years.

My response to her? A lie. I told her that it was good, knowing deep down inside that it was just awful, but I could not bring myself to tell her what had actually happened. She accepted that answer and did not ask again. In hindsight, I wish I would have told the truth then. I so very much regret that to this date.

We continued to see each other. She came to McGraw one day and I showed her how to play racquetball. She turned out to be a natural and I was really impressed. We would get together and play as often as time allowed. It was great fun.

After an afternoon of playing racquetball, we decided to go for a walk. She told me she went to church and she was an active member there. Again, my thought was, *where will this lead?* And my next thought was just to walk away from this all, Hannah included. I just did not want the past to repeat itself. I was torn apart as I had begun to develop feelings for her.

I poured myself more and more into my work, sports, and giving springboard diving lessons. These kept my mind off so many things. It was, mentally, a very difficult time for me.

One day, Hannah asked me if wanted to meet her parents. Again, another alarm went off telling me, *Parents again?* After my experience with my own parents and foster parents, I just did not want to run the risk of going through something like that all over again. But something inside nudged me to accept the invitation. We agreed that I would come to her house on the weekend.

On that day, I was very tense, sweating profusely, very worried, and my mind was spinning with scenarios of what all could go wrong and that the past would return again.

I arrived at her house. I got out of the car and rang the doorbell. Hannah answered it and slightly stepped forward to give me a hug. I think I took a short step backwards as I was not expecting that. I allowed her to do that and it was a very short hug, but it was not all that bad. Actually, it felt good.

She asked me to come into her parents' apartment. We entered and went to the dining room. I immediately noticed that the place was immaculate and the table was very nicely set with lit candles. In the middle of the table was, you can guess it, a cheesecake. Hannah said that the cake was prepared by her mother, whose eyes I then made contact with, followed by her father's.

Hannah introduced us and we exchanged handshakes. Their hands were very warm and dry, mine cold and soaking wet from being so nervous. I begin to think about what I was doing here. So many thoughts were racing through my mind. It felt like a small panic attack.

Her mother signaled us to join them for cake and tea, the same tea that I drank the first time I met Hannah. Her parents appeared to be very nice. They knew I was an American. What they did not know, and Hannah having not told them in advance, is that I had learned to speak German. After the cake and tea were served, her parents, in their best English, were making polite and conversation. I liked their accents and answered in English.

This went on for a while, until her mother asked how I liked Germany and if I had been able to learn some German. I chuckled inside as both of them almost fell out of their chairs when I answered the question completely in German. They both had big smiles on their faces. They were truly surprised, not only by that, but that their daughter had not let them in the secret. Her mother laughed and commented that we had managed to pull one over on them. We all laughed. I winked at Hannah for pulling off this feat with me. I realized that my hands had become warm and dry.

We had a very pleasant afternoon together. I liked both of them, and it was very hard for me to hide my envy and jealousy inside knowing that their daughter had been raised so well by such wonderful parents. They both told me that I was welcome back at any time. They were very kind. I did, though, have the thought, *well, if only they knew the real me inside*.

A few days later, I was on a long run and begin to think more about Hannah, not just as a friend, but perhaps more.

I recalled the conversation that I had with my boss that in order to climb the career ladder, I should get married and have children.

I struggled greatly with this. All that had happened in the past came rushing in again. My question to myself was, *just exactly what are you trying to do here, and who are you trying to please?* This whole thing just was at the front of my thoughts. I masked all my worries, not letting on to anyone what was going on inside of me, including Hannah.

My thoughts were also on a God whom I thought hated me, that I was never chosen to be part of His family and predestined for hell. I said this thinking about all the times I got told to go to hell and the hate I was so often exposed to. I questioned if I was ever loved by them or anyone else at all, including God. And then the huge and gut-wrenching battle about my own sexuality.

With Carolyn wanting to make me into a girl, and with all of the same-sex abuse, it had me questioning if I was born into the wrong body, just a freak of nature? And yes, I entertained thoughts of changing my gender. It was all just too much.

My thoughts did turn to my parents and foster parents. I must say, even with all that happened and the times that I thought I disliked them so much, I guess I never really stopped loving them. For me, I wanted to love, be loved, and to respect them, but after seeing no love displayed, I convinced myself that this is what love was supposed to be like. And so I wound up turning on myself with a great level of self-loathing and hate, and absolutely no love for myself whatsoever.

It was so excruciatingly painful for me, and so as it related to Hannah and her parents, this display of another kind of love was foreign to me. Would they, ultimately, turn on me and reject me as well?

But the real struggle I was facing was that I begin to question my own motives as to what is that I really want out of my life. And with no one to talk to and with my general lack of trust in people, it made it even more difficult for me.

Hannah and I continued to see each other and our relationship grew and yes, my feelings for her were getting stronger. But I was terrified in going any farther, after having what I went through in my childhood and everything else that traumatically happened to me. A part of me said that I should not pursue this.

But, from a worldly point of view, I continued to weigh more and more what my boss had told me. He even entrusted me a bit about his own story and also having decided to get married in the beginning of his career so he could climb the ladder and achieve success.

He did, and so he became a bit of an example, or perhaps encouragement for me. My biggest fear was not primarily about getting married, but with the potential of having children. I did not want to put another child through what I had experienced, and I was terrified that I would repeat the same mistakes that I went through so long ago.

But at the same time, I wanted to climb the ladder, I wanted to have success, and I wanted to make it. I wanted it all. I just wanted it my way.

The more I considered this, the more I thought, *well, Chase, why don't you just try it out? If you give it a chance, it might just work out—being in love, getting married, and perhaps having children.*

At the same time, and in the very forefront of my mind, I knew so much about her, and yet she knew so little about me. There was so much guilt and shame, and more importantly, I did not want to be rejected and abandoned again, and even hurt someone I cared for very much. I was really messed up.

But with my desire to be a "somebody" in the military, and being so driven to please but at the same time also being so selfish and prideful, in the final analysis, I chose to give it a try.

We did not have much of a courtship. We dated for a couple of months. One evening, I asked her out to dinner at the *Waldeslust*. I was very nervous and still questioning my motives, but managed, with yet another mask on, to hide this from Hannah.

I told her after dinner that I had ordered dessert for us and that it would be something she knew and also one of her favorites. She looked very happy and said that she was very curious.

I signaled the waiter, whom I had arranged with in advance, to serve the desert, which turned out to be a cheesecake created by the pastry chef. He personally brought it to the table with a lit candle in the middle. Herbal tea was also served.

She looked at both, looked at me, and said, "This is so sweet of you, you remembered."

I told her that her cheesecake and tea had left a wonderful impression on me and that I wanted to reciprocate. At my signal, the pastry chef sliced the cake and served it to us.

We were enjoying the cake and the tea. I noticed that Hannah was taking small bites of the cake. I just kept watching when she took another bite. Suddenly, she stopped chewing when she realized that there was something in the cake.

She had a very puzzled look on her face as she took her napkin to remove what was in her mouth. She quickly realized that what was in the piece of cake was a ring. I was thankful that she did not swallow it.

She looked at it and took it in her napkin and wiped it clean. I was humored at her response, which was, "Oh, the pastry chef must have lost her ring!"

I told her that I did not think that was the case. I got up from my seat and walked to her seat, picked up the ring, and got down on my knee. I asked her if she would like to get married, and she blurted out, "Yes! Yes! Yes!" and "I love you so much and want to spend the rest of my life with you."

My thought was *OK, you did it, now see if you can make this work.* I did not like myself much at all for what was supposed to be a magic moment, but I will confess I know this is horrible, that I was already on the first step of that career ladder. Deception was taking its root. How very sad.

She did tell me, though, that she would have to talk to her parents. I told her that this was a good idea.

Her parents were active in their church. Her father served as an elder and her mother as a teacher in the women's ministry. I had shared with them some interesting discussions about Christianity, faith, and belief. Her father would ask me probing questions about my own faith, and I managed to convince him that I was "saved." Oh, going back those so many years to Reverend Moore. By this time, I was attending their church. I liked the services and mostly the messages that were preached. It was pretty easy getting along with the other church members, and I guess being engaged to an elder's daughter helped in that.

I recall one conversation that Hannah and I had with her parents about the subject of marriage. He told me that he was looking forward to his daughter finding a fine, upstanding Christian man who loved Jesus, practiced following Him, and was a man of faith, truth, and of good Christian character. Again, my thought was just to flee. Why didn't I? I was on a mission—starting to climb that ladder.

He held a Bible study with Hannah, me, and her mother. It was based in Romans 12, in which Paul spelled out the marks of a "true Christian." Her father even went so far to take these passages and turn them into a type of report card, like we all received going through school. The exercise was to look at each of the marks listed and then give Yourself a grade for each mark.

THE HOLLOW MASK

It was a very interesting study, but it scared me tremendously because I did not even know if I was a Christian at that point, or perhaps just wearing another mask and trying to fit in. I took the test.

I believe that this was the first time that I really attempted to look deep within myself. The missed marks: I say this as in the Hebrew, the word for sin is *khata*, meaning "to fail" or to "miss the mark." We were taught this in Sunday school.

From love being genuine, to abhorring evil and holding fast to what is good, to truly loving others, to honoring them, to rejoicing in hope, to blessing those who are against me, and to being prideful; well, it was overwhelming.

Being an otherwise overachiever and getting very good grades in school, these grades were a resounding failure, for me worse than an F-. It made me think back to when I qualified as an expert with the M16 Rifle; there I hit all the targets just perfectly. But here?

I lied to her father when he asked how I did on the test. I said, "Not too bad, but I have some work to do."

He seemed to accept that and responded, "We all do." Hanna and I did not speak about the test.

It made me start to wonder if, in fact, I could even begin to truly possess any of these marks. Being the perfectionist that I had become, and always wanting to have absolute control, and be the best and to please everyone, I did, though, often think that I had become morally bankrupt and that there was no chance for me, Christian or not.

As for Hannah and her parents, they seemed to possess all of these marks—in my mind anyway. What appeared to come from them was from hearts full of love and caring. I was, nonetheless, very suspicious and finding trust very hard.

After the study, I was completely in the dumps. But we planned to have dinner together, so I stayed. It was a good meal with *Schweinsbraten*, potato dumplings, and red cabbage (or 'Blaukraut' in Bavaria), which became one of my favorite German meals. Afterwards, we had tea and cake.

After the meal, her father served us glasses of champagne. Surprisingly, his toast was to Hannah and me, that he and his wife wished us a long and blessed life together, bound together in Christ. I remember he quoted Colossians 3:14: "And over all these virtues put on love, which is the bond of perfect unity." Those words sounded good to me, and inwardly I wished I would have taken them more seriously.

I was surprised because I did not even have the opportunity to ask his daughter's hand in marriage. He then stated, to my great surprise, that he and his wife knew in their hearts and were convinced that I was a fine Christian man, and that I would be perfect for their daughter. And he followed up by telling us that we have both his and his wife's blessing.

I had never in my life had anyone told me such positive things and in such a loving manner. But I immediately questioned myself, "*A fine young Christian man who would be perfect for their daughter? Had I become, with all those masks, the ultimate "show master"?*

With the engagement and the approval of her parents to get married, we began planning for the wedding. Thoughts were still going through my mind as to what I was doing and if I was even sure that this is what I really wanted or desired. But to me, these people were, at the time, very loving and caring people, who welcomed me into their family and lives. It was something I had been yearning for all my life.

We decided that we wanted to get married in late spring. We spoke about so many things, including sexual relations. I knew Hannah believed that sexual relations belonged within a marriage, and that she was saving herself for marriage. With what had happened to me throughout my life up until now with sex, and now with her "puritan" beliefs (or so I thought), I considered myself to be more than damaged goods. I was being just selfish—she deserved better.

One evening, we went out to dinner and had a very good time and another great meal. We had a bit too much to drink and when we drove back to her place, she asked me in. I wanted to decline and go back to the barracks, but she convinced me to come in. We found ourselves sitting on the sofa in her living room holding hands. And then, we started kissing.

As we looked at each other, she said, "Chase, I know what God's Word says about having sex before marriage, and my desire was to keep myself until that day, but I also know that I am truly and completely in love with you." That caught me completely off guard, and it did not take long for me to see where this all was going. She told me that she wanted to have sex with me.

This time, it was much different from any of the other times I had experienced. It was tender and loving, but afterwards, my mind was reeling with the thought of what had just happened. I was also very concerned about Hannah and how she felt. She told me that it was very nice and that she had no regrets about doing it.

It surprised me to hear that, but at the same time, I experienced firsthand with myself what excessive alcohol consumption did to affect my senses and desires, not to mention the music in the background and being there alone together. I thought that I would be strong enough to resist this, but I was not, and the result filled me with shame and regret. I wish I had not have gone into her apartment and instead returned to the barracks.

And then the shame and regret came in another form, in that I should have been completely honest with her from the beginning, but I was not. Instead, I continued to hide behind countless masks.

I told her that I needed to get back to the barracks to prepare for a project for the next day. Another lie. It was a rather short good bye, but I just had to flee. I took a taxi back to the barracks, so confused, full of shame and regret. I was completely in turmoil, all of which came from my own doing. I wondered just how much more I could take. Thinking that I was morally bankrupt, I tried to push this as far in the back of my mind with so many other events.

A thought occurred to me in that I remember learning in Sunday School that "sin keeps us out of the Bible, but the Bible keeps us out of sin". Before I turned off the nightstand light, I saw my Bible. I took it and "hid it" in the drawer. It stayed there for a good while. I did not sleep that night.

Hannah and I spoke the next day. She asked me how I was doing. I told her I was doing okay—another lie. I then asked her the same question and she said that she was feeling good, that she loved me, and was looking forward to marrying me, spending the rest of our lives together. Her statement unsettled me because I did not even know if I knew what real love and faithfulness was. Why could I just not tell her the truth?

Had that advice my boss gave gotten so much into me that I was basically following those words to a T? I found myself again about to make a very important decision without really thinking about the consequences. What was wrong with me? I was a mess, a "man-made disaster."

We agreed to meet after work that day. I admit that I did not really want to meet because, with the past, I was scared that I was about to be set up again like with Teri, Linda, and Lisa. With Hannah, I thought like I had hoped before, that maybe this time it would be different.

The first few moments were awkward because I really did not know what to say. Hannah sensed this and took my hand and told me that everything will be okay. She said that we love each other and that this would see us through. She also assured me that she was here for me and to take care of me and that I should not worry about anything. Where did I hear that before? I managed to tell her that I was here for her as well, although not knowing for sure in my heart if I would follow through with that.

Time went by. I was working, she was working. I was also involved in my studies and giving diving lessons. It was hard for me to concentrate on much because of what had happened between us. I could not bring myself to talk to anyone about this, including Michi.

One day at work, I received a phone call from Hannah. I immediately sensed that she was not her usual calm self. I asked her what was wrong and her response was that we needed to meet after work. I thought to myself, not again—*another betrayal or rejection?*

When we met after work, I asked her what she wanted to drink and she answered, "Just water." I ordered her a water and myself a beer. When the beverages were served, I raised my glass in a toast. Her response took me completely by surprise. She simply said, "We are going to have a baby."

I was stunned. My mind immediately started racing and my heartbeat shot through the roof. I quickly tried to regain my composure and as best as I could with yet another mask on. I smiled, trying to open my eyes a bit wider, and said, "Wow, that's great news!" I then asked if her parents knew. She told me that she wanted me to be the first to hear this. This frightened me as I knew that they were very devout people.

Hannah continued, telling me she was around six weeks pregnant and that she was so looking forward to having a child with me. I feigned happiness as best as I could, but inside I was in torture. I did not ever in a million years expect this. What had I done? I knew I was not even ready to have a child, most likely because of the child that was still in me—very abused, rejected, scorned, and abandoned.

We spent, what turned out to be a blur for me, the evening with her being so excited and going on about a name, baby room, nationalities, language, schools, sports, university, and careers. This was all too much for me, but for her sake, I tried to positively participate in the discussion.

After parting ways, I arrived at the barracks and collapsed into bed. Like so many times before, so many thoughts happening, with my primary thought being, *Chase, what on earth did you do now?*

I then steeled myself to come clean with her about my past, something I regret not doing before. I had to do this soonest. I just did not want to go on hiding behind all the lies, the deception, the masks. She deserved to know the truth and I had absolute responsibility to tell her that truth.

I had no idea about how to go about doing this, except just to sit her down and confess it all to her.

But I thought I needed help. So, I contacted the pastor of the church and asked for meeting with him. He said that I could come by.

I went there after work. He could sense that something was wrong, but did not begin by probing and asking questions. He prayed for our meeting. After that, he gave me a glass of water and we sat there in silence.

I started speaking and wound up telling him my life's story, ending with confessing that Hannah was pregnant. Expecting from him damnation, rejection, and "you are going to hell," he looked at me with tears in his eyes, took my hands into his, and said, "You are very courageous for sharing this with me. You went through a lot of very difficult and painful times. You have held all of these in for so long, and I am proud of you for doing this now. But know this, Chase: God is love, He is merciful, He is gracious, and He is forgiving. He knows Your past, He saw what you went through, including the bad choices you ever made, are making, and will ever make."

I could say no more. I was empty. He told me there is a Bible verse in Proverbs 28:18, which says that "he who hides his sins shall not prosper, but he who confesses them and renounces them will find forgiveness." I conveniently tucked this verse into the back of my mind.

He also said, "Your parents and foster parents should have nurtured and cared for you, but they did not do that. That is something they will have to answer for. From what you told me, you were not to blame."

This was hard for me to comprehend as I always thought it was my fault that I was not a good child to them.

We then discussed how I would go about revealing this all to Hannah.

I told him that I honestly did not have the courage to do this on my own. He offered to invite Hannah and me to his office. That sounded like a reasonable plan to me. He then prayed for me, for Hannah, and also for himself for God's wisdom and the leading of the Holy Spirit and then, lastly, he prayed for the baby in Hannah's womb. I also found myself praying this same thing. I broke down in tears.

When I mentioned the meeting to Hannah, she assumed we would be going to a premarital counseling session. I did not let on what we would be talking about. I just could not bring myself to do it. That, in my mind, made me an even worse person. After all, this is the woman who is carrying our baby and also who I planned to marry.

We met with the pastor a couple of days later. I was so nervous, again sweating with cold, damp hands. I had absolutely no idea what would transpire. The pastor then prayed as he did before, especially for the Lord's guiding Spirit to be among us.

I will mention here that even with as much time I spent in the Bible, and also referencing it many times, I was not a believer. I heard what was said and taught to me, but taking that step of "being born again" I had not.

Looking back now, I saw myself like the Pharisees whom Jesus confronted in Matthew 23:27, where He graphically told them (I took the liberty of personalizing this verse for me). "Woe to you, Chase, you hypocrite! For you are like a whitewashed tomb (another mask), which outwardly appears beautiful, but within is filled of dead bones and all uncleanness." With my ever so important need to please people, at times at a very high cost, I most likely subconsciously try to do this with God as well.

I had, I supposed, become very legalistic in the sense of trying to obtain some "brownie points" in God's and others' eyes through my good works. Perhaps, this all could positively affect my standing with God and make me believe that through all that, I could earn my salvation. How wrong I turned out to be about this. I earlier wrote about grace and faith, two concepts I had not even begin to grasp up until this point. As I wrote earlier, my head knowledge was strong, my heart so full of pride, and my ego huge. I remember a brother one day stating in church, "Ego out, Jesus in." That made some sense to me. I knew that things had to change, and drastically.

Returning to our meeting, the pastor sensed my inward dread. He turned to Hannah and said that he believed that I needed to confess something to her. I immediately noticed the puzzled look on her face. That made me even more ashamed and feeling so dirty.

I inhaled a deep breath, held it, and then exhaled it with pursed lips. I looked at Hannah and told her that the pastor was right about wanting to confess something to her. She said, "OK, please do so."

I went on to tell her all of what I had told the pastor. I was terrified, I was shaking, and what I really wanted to do was to just—as on so many occasions before—flee. But this time was different. There was a child.

She listened very intently and her emotions changed with mine. I told her that I was very sorry for not sharing this with her, confessing to lying and deception. I begged her for forgiveness. She looked me very lovingly, took my hands in hers, and told me that she was very sorry for what happened and could, in some way, understand, why I did not share all of this before.

She then said, "The past is the past; we all have one. Even with what you just shared, and bravely at that, my feelings and love for you will not change. I forgive you, Chase."

This was a definite shock to me, as such a reaction was so rare for me.

I began crying uncontrollably on her shoulder. It felt as if such a great burden was finally lifted. At the same time, I was so thankful that she forgave me. I looked up at her and simply said, "Thank you." To me, this was what a Christian life should look like. I remembered the evening with her and her parents in Romans 12, the marks of a true Christian and letting love be genuine—perhaps I did need to greatly change and improve those grades..

It felt so good to finally open up and tell the truth. But I still was struggling with the thought of becoming a husband and a father. At some point, I said to myself, *OK, Chase, this is it. This is the acceptance that you have been looking for all Your life. And don't go screwing this up.* Could I actually achieve that? But nonetheless, the voices of the past kept creeping in—*You will never amount to anything.*

I went forward with Hannah. One thing that was crystal-clear for me—I did not want this child to go through all what I had been through. This is something I would not wish upon my worst enemy.

We continued with the wedding plans, venues, invitations, etc. We decided to go shopping and look for baby furniture and other items. We had discussed that after getting married, I would move in with Hannah. Her apartment had an extra room that we planned on converting into a nursery.

A few weeks later, we were at church. I was thinking that no one there—with the exception of the pastor, Hannah, and myself—knew that she was pregnant. And I was wondering how that news would be accepted, especially from her parents. I had spoken to Hannah on a couple of occasions about letting her parents know, but she chose not to do that. I wondered if they had suspected anything.

And I resolved in that moment that I wanted to truly see this through. This was my new mission, one that I hoped would finally turn out positively.

In the middle of a sermon, I was startled to hear Hannah wince in pain. I turned to her and asked her if everything was okay. She said she wasn't feeling so good. I asked her if she wanted to leave and she said no. I edged closer to her and took her hand, holding it tightly. But the pain became stronger and she clutched my hand very tightly. There was a doctor friend sitting in the pew behind us and I turned to him for help. He had already noticed that Hannah was in pain. I whispered to him and asked him if he would go with us out of the room.

Hannah barely made it to the hallway before she collapsed into my arms. I was so afraid—I realized she was unconscious. I did not know what was wrong. Someone called for an ambulance and it arrived very quickly. I rode in the ambulance with her, still holding her hand.

Sadly, Hannah suffered a miscarriage in the church hallway. I was devastated beyond anything I had ever felt in my life. I could not fathom what had happened. And then my thoughts turned back to Lisa. With intent, she aborted an unwanted child. Lisa had acted as though nothing really tragic had occurred. But here, this baby's life was ended due to other causes. And I would not think about aborting this baby, even if it was conceived out of wedlock. We both wanted this child and were very excited about it.

I was at Hannah's side when she regained consciousness. She looked at me, dazed, and without me even saying a word, asked, "Did we lose the baby?" All I could do was keep holding her hand. I told her that I was so sorry. Both hers and my heart were broken as each of us struggled to fathom why this had happened.

We sat there for a good period of time in silence. We had not spoken since she had asked if we had lost the baby. Hannah was lost in her own thoughts, me as well.

After a long period of silence, I asked Hannah how she was. She did not respond other than to turn her face away. In that moment, it became all too much for me. I asked Hannah if it would be okay if I stepped out of the room and go to the toilet (once again, perhaps to flee?). She signaled that it would be okay, and so I left the room.

I was on my way back to her room when I saw a sign for a chapel. I followed that sign around the corner and I entered the chapel. It was empty. I was there all by myself and so I went to the front pew and found myself standing in front of the cross. As I looked up at it, I said, "God, or whoever, why did this happen? Why did everything in my life turn out bad? You saw the severe trauma, pain, and rejection that I had gone through, and now this; was it all not enough? Why, why?" In that moment, I did not think about sinning and that decisions have consequences. I simply turned and walked away.

When I arrived back in Hannah's room, her parents were there. My first thought is that they would have been very concerned about their daughter. And I could see that they were. But the statement that her mother made to me (with a pointing finger) was, "You are to blame. We hold you responsible for this baby's death. You should be ashamed of Yourself, putting our family through so much pain and turmoil."

How could they have said this, and what grounds were they basing that on? I was absolutely stunned by this direct attack.

In her weakened condition, Hannah attempted to tell her mother to stop and that this was not the case. She said that she loved me and this was not my fault, and that we would get through this together. She asked her mother to leave me alone. But her mother, who I thought was very loving and very kind, basically ordered both Hannah and me to keep silent. Her father, who had not said anything until then, turned to me and said, "We think that it would be best if you just go."

I shouted out in anger and confusion, "I did not do anything, why are you blaming me? Let me be with Hannah." I tried to get to Hannah's bed, but her father stepped in and blocked me. I cried out to Hannah, "Please, help me. We can get through this together." I frantically tried to capture a glance from Hannah, but her mother was bent over her and cradling her face, which was turned away from me. I picked up my coat, turned around, slammed the door, and walked out.

I wandered aimlessly for hours on end. I was just trying to wrap my head around what had just happened. I did not think, even in my wildest imagination, that this—what should have been a very special time—so suddenly unraveled in front of my eyes.

How was Hannah doing? What thoughts were going through her mind? When would I be able to see her again? I wanted to be by her side so much—I did not want her to be alone. This happened to me so many times. And what got into her parents? I was still in shock from what they said to me. I started to wonder how it would go from here.

And what about the future? That "career ladder", now seemed so unimportant. But after having that brief thought, in that moment, I could care less about that.

I managed to get back to the barracks and tried to contact the hospital to inquire about Hannah. I was told that only immediate family members would be privy to that information. I told the lady on the phone that I was the father of the child. She repeated her previous statement. I tried on multiple occasions to get through, but each time I was told no. How can it be that the father of the child was not permitted to find out what was happening? Was Hannah blaming me as her mother did? What was going on in there? I started to get angry.

I just existed, going through the motions. I lost interest in just about everything, including the reason for my wanting to come to Germany—springboard diving.

Michi called me one day and said that he had not heard from me and wanted to check in with me. He could tell that something was wrong. He did not ask me what that was, but he said that he would come over to see me after he was finished at work. He arrived later in the afternoon. He knew right away that something was wrong and asked me about what was going on.

I was not feeling well at all. My heart was racing yet again, and I was shaking and sweating uncontrollably. He said that it would be good to go and see a doctor. He said that the doctor is good friend of his, a neurologist and psychiatrist. He called and the receptionist told us to come right away.

Michi drove me there. On the way to the doctor's office, he asked me what was wrong. I told him in broken sentences what had happened with Hannah, and her parents telling me to go away. He shook his head in disbelief. He put his hand on my shoulder and told me, "God and I are here for you, my friend." He would prove to be an absolute wonderful, faithful, and loyal friend. I will write more about him later.

At the doctor's office, they immediately took me into treatment room. I said that I wanted to have Michi there. The doctor allowed that. They hooked me up to a heart and pulse monitor and then administered an EKG. My stats were off the charts. I felt as though I was going to implode.

She asked me what symptoms I was experiencing and I told her I was feeling overwhelmed, unable to concentrate, burnt out, angry, and full of rage. So many things in my life were racing through my mind, and then now this with Hannah. It was not good.

She inserted an IV and proceeded to pump Adenocor into my body, which, according to her, would slow down the electrical impulses controlling my heart rhythm, which would then lower the rhythm, returning it to normal levels.

After the Adenocor kicked in, my heart and pulse stats decreased steadily. The doctor also administered an injection of Lorazepam (Tavor), used to relieve anxiety due to temporary situational stress (this time around, I actually gladly accepted them). Lorazepam is a benzodiazepine and works by slowing activity in the brain to allow for relaxation.

All of that put me to sleep. When I awoke, a nurse was there, along with Michi. I felt much better. I asked how long I had slept and Michi said it was close to eight hours.

The nurse notified the doctor that I was awake. She came by to check on me. She told me that, in her medical opinion, I had suffered a nervous breakdown. She asked if I knew what could have caused this. I just shrugged my shoulders, silently assigning the blame to me.

She told me that I should stay there for an hour for more observation and that if my stats returned to normal, I should be discharged later on. She did tell me that I needed rest, lots of it. She gave me my very first German sick slip. It called for ten days of complete rest. I wondered how this would be accepted by my office. I was scheduled to be at work next morning. The doctor said that she had cases with the military like this before, and that I should submit the sick slip to my superiors.

All symptoms had returned to normal by the late afternoon, and I was released. Michi drove me back to the barracks. We entered the barracks and the CQ was sitting at his desk. I handed him the sick slip and briefly explained what happened. The CQ said that he was not familiar with a German sick slip and would have to contact his supervisor.

I introduced Michi to him as my friend. I had my own room, and asked if Michi could remain overnight at the barracks. The

CQ had the authority to grant overnight stays, and he said it would be okay. The CQ instructed me that if any symptoms were to return, he should be contacted immediately.

We went to my room. I just flopped myself on to the bed. Michi served us both a glass of water. I was just completely exhausted and totally worn out. I thanked Michi for going through all of this with me and he once again said that he would be here for me.

We did not talk much that evening, with the exception of his telling me that he would take leave to stay with me. He offered me to stay at his place. I thanked him and told him I would talk to my boss about this. It really was good to have him there. Without him, I would otherwise find myself being alone yet again.

Before saying good night, I told Michi that we can speak about things in the morning. I also told him that I hoped Hannah was doing better. I was so worried but tried not to get overly worked up about this. She was so much on my mind.

I thought about what she implied when she turned her face away from me in the hospital room—or was it her mother turning her head to the side? And why did her parents react the way that they did? I ask myself these because what I witnessed from them was pure meanness.

Perhaps, it was their way of initially dealing with news of two events, a pregnancy and a miscarriage. I could not imagine how hard that must have hit them. Hannah was just not ready to tell them. So much was going through my mind. But I needed rest. I took the prescribed Lorazepam tablet and managed to fall asleep fairly quickly.

Morning came quickly. There was a knock on the door. It was my boss. He had been informed by the CQ of what happened. He asked me how I was doing.

This time, I told the truth and said I was not doing so well. He responded by telling me that he had the sick slip from the German doctor and saw that I had suffered a nervous breakdown. He said to me to get the prescribed rest and that we would discuss this later. I wondered what that meant.

He told me that I must follow her directions to get complete rest. I asked him if I could take those days by staying with my friend, Michi, who I introduced him to. I told my boss that the attending doctor is a friend of his, and also that he did not live too far away. My boss agreed, and he and Michi exchanged telephone numbers and the address where I would be staying. My boss asked to be kept informed of my progress.

It was so kind of Michi to let me stay with him. He packed my things together and I checked out at the CQ desk. We drove to Michi's apartment. He had a very nice place with two bedrooms and bathrooms. It was good to be with him.

We spent time talking about so many things. I told him more about what had happened in my life. He said that it was awful what happened to me. He said that he was very sorry for me. Little by little, I found myself sharing my life with him. He listened with great interest. I said I knew he was a Christian, but that I was not really interested in the "born again" thing, and especially with what happened with Hannah and being blamed by, in my mind, "so called" Christians that I was at fault for her miscarriage. I was full of hatred towards them.

I tried several times, without success, to find out about Hannah by calling her and her parent's numbers. I was so worried about her and still did not know why she stopped speaking with me. This time, it really hurt as I was the father of that child. I was wondering if the child would be buried. I did not even get to know the gender of the baby. It was devastating to me.

The doctor visited with me several times and asked questions about my past as well as having me complete two questionnaires about my health. After reviewing them, she diagnosed me with complex posttraumatic stress disorder (PTSD) and borderline personality disorder (BPD).

I knew a little about PTSD but almost nothing about BPD. She told me BPD was a serious, and most likely, long-lasting and complex mental health issue. She went on to explain that BPD is a disorder that severely impacts a person's ability to manage their emotions and that this loss of emotional control can increase impulsivity, affecting how a person feels about themselves. The disorder also leads to negatively impacting their relationships with others. People who suffer from the disorder tend to have an intense fear of abandonment or instability, and want to be alone in order to reduce the possibility of abandonment.

I said, "Just from those two questionnaires you were able to diagnose me with these two disorders?" She answered affirmatively. I asked her what could be done and she stated that there are therapies that can be prescribed. My heart and pulse rate were up as I did not know how to process all of these. It was like a nightmare that I could not wake up from. I said thank you and told her I just wanted to be alone. *Oh*, I said to myself, *wanting to be alone? That might be a sign.*

Michi was there with me. He was sorry to learn of this, and that, once again, he stated that he would be there for me. I just took my medicine and went to sleep.

Towards the end of my sick leave, the doctor came again. She took my stats and told me that they were a bit better, that the Tavor was aiding in this, along with Zopiclone to aid in sleeping.

I told her that I was very worried about Hannah and how she was doing. She told me this was one of the reasons she came to see me this time. My mind was already racing thinking about what she wanted to tell me.

She said that she had spoken to Hannah's parents and also visited briefly with Hannah. I asked her how Hannah was doing and she told me that she was doing okay under the circumstances. Before I could reply and asked if they had mentioned me, she told me that neither Hannah nor her parents wanted to see me again. I asked why.

She said that it would be best for all involved, including the church, and they hoped that this would just go away.

"Go away, for them—what about me?" I asked in a loud voice. "This just cannot go away!"

She said that the church decided that this would be in their best interest. As she herself was a member of that church, I asked her if she thought this was in their best interest. Before she could reply and with the look on her face, I waved my hand, signaling I did not want to have a response.

I was furious. "How can the church decide this without even taking me into account? I am the father of that child. I have a right to know! And why is this a decision of the church?"

She said, "You know that her father is elder at the church, and her mother was a teacher. And with what had happened with Hannah, you know, the "grave sinning", along with Your mental health being so fragile, they asked also that in Your best interest, please do not pursue this."

Her last statement about that situation was "we have concluded that it would be better for you to not attend our church again and that you should stop trying to contact Hannah." And this statement coming from a doctor and "supposed" sister in Christ?

I said, "My best interest? How do they know what my best interest is? And what about Hannah's 'serious sinning?'" And they sent you as the harbinger of bad news? I cannot believe this." I added, "I have had it with the church. They had closed ranks to protect shield the church and most their positions there. By doing so, they chose to deal with me by simply rejecting and abandoning me yet again."

She did not respond to my statement. She brought more Tavor with her, along with Zopiclone. She also gave me a sick slip for ten additional days.

Michi was in the room all this time. I said, "This is not the first time this has happened with the church. As with then, and now, they are making me feel like I am a leper. It is like they put me on trial in absentia! Are they all so perfect? What about all the love, grace, mercy, and forgiveness that Jesus taught, and also with those marks of a 'true Christian' in Romans 12 that believers should be striving to live out. It all looked like a cover up to me. It was, as we called it in the military 'closing ranks.' I want nothing to do with religion, ever again!"

Michi was sitting on the bed, tearing up, and said, "I am very sorry for what the church did to you, Chase. That was not right. But I will tell you, Our Heavenly Father is not looking for religion, He is looking for a relationship."

I replied, "When I look back at my father and foster father, I wanted nothing to do with them, especially having a relationship." Perhaps, this is how I felt about the "Heavenly Father"?

Michi stood up, went over to the dressing drawer, opened it, and pulled out a brown bag. He returned to my bedside and handed me the bag. I opened it. It was the plaque from the chief with the verse from Isaiah, "See, I will not forget you for I have carved Your name on the palms of my hands." I looked at it and then at Michi.

He said, "Chase, this is one of over 7,000 promises from God in the Bible. He has not failed to fulfill one of His promises to date. And He has not forgotten you, I promise you that."

I said thank you and placed the plaque on the nightstand.

Still, I was more than devastated. Why? And now the church again rejecting me? I remember hearing a long time ago that Christians cannot be mentally ill, and even if they could be, it was most likely due to demonic influences and strongholds. I remember being infuriated with that message then; it just rubbed me the wrong way. Are only healthy Christians the ones who are accepted, and now, if a Christian does become mentally ill, it has to be because of a demon? I remember hearing that Jesus had made the statement that it is not the well ones who need a doctor, but the sick ones.

I knew there was something wrong with me; there was no doubt about that. I thought to myself, *this is crazy*. My next thought was, w*hat would Jesus think of my situation, and what of those with mental illnesses that He chose to heal? Could he choose to heal me?* The plaque seemed to imply that. Even with all of what just happened, I just threw my hands up in the air in disgust.

Unfortunately, things turned for the worse with my mental state. I just could not go on any longer. I called the doctor and told her how bad things had become and that I just wanted it all to end. This was hard for me to do, because of all of what she had told me about what the church had said. There was no trust any longer. She told me that, in her medical opinion, I needed immediate psychiatric help, especially if I was thinking about taking my life.

I asked her what that meant and she told me that I immediately needed to be admitted to a psychiatric ward. I said not so nicely to her, "Perhaps Your whole church would do good in seeking psychiatric help."

At that point, I really did not have much fighting left in me, so I reluctantly told her that I would go there, but also said that I did not really think this would help. She said that she would call them and advise them that I was coming and that an admission order would be waiting there for me.

After that call, I told Michi about what had happened. He said that he agreed with the doctor as my condition had become much worse. He said that I would get the professional help I needed there. He helped me put a few belongings together and he drove me there.

When we arrived, the admission order was there. I was escorted into a room. Michi was there with me. The doctor came in and introduced himself. He told me that he had spoken to my doctor and that she informed him about my condition. He then asked me if I had plans to harm myself, and I told him that I was having thoughts about ending my life.

He told me that I was in the right place. He said that he arranged a station for me for admission, but it would take a bit of time. He asked me to go back to the waiting room. As I was sitting there with Michi, I told him that he could return back to his place and I would contact him as soon as I was able to.

He reluctantly did this and told me that he would be praying for me. We hugged and he left.

After a while, the doctor returned and called me into his office. He said that the station was ready to accept me. In that moment, I had a change of mind. I lied and told him that I was doing much better and that I decided I did not want to be admitted. He advised me that I should stay, but that he could not force me to stay there. And I left, with my belongings, along with the medicine I had been prescribed.

I did not contact Michi. I recalled seeing his church that we passed while driving to the clinic. I walked there. I entered and, just as it happened while at the hospital with Hannah, I was alone. I approached the front stood in front of the Cross. I wondered why I was back at a church after walking out of the chapel at the Hospital and then making my mind up that I wanted nothing to do with religion. What kept me coming back?

I sat down and took my journal out of my backpack. I started writing. When I had finished, I realized that I had just composed a suicide note. I had decided to do it and this time succeed. I noticed that there was a visitor's book near the altar. I wrote a short note basically saying that I cannot carry on any longer and asked for whoever would read this to pray for my soul. There was a stand next to the altar with burning candles. I took a new one, lit it, and then left. I was on a new mission, hopefully my last.

I walked for a while and saw a liquor store. I purchased two large bottles of whisky and walked back to the church, this time to the back garden, where there was a shed. I checked to see if it was locked, but it was not. I entered and in it was a lawn mower, other gardening tools, and a garden chair. I wondered why it was left open. It was also fairly chilly there, and all I had on for protection was a light jacket. I thought that perhaps this was "a meant to be" with the shed door being open.

I sat down on the chair and I took the medicines (Tavor and Zopiclone) out of my backpack. I also remembered that my Bible was in there too. I noticed something else was there. It was the bag with the plaque in it. I took it out as well. Michi must have placed it there.

I opened the bottle of whisky and began taking tablet by tablet, swallowing them with the whisky. I was angry at the church and how they had rejected me. I was angry with Hannah and her parents who did not want to have anything to do with me. I was angry at so many other people and what they did to me.

And now, finding myself angry with God as well, I took the plaque in my hands, raised it up, and as though He was standing there, which I doubted, I said in a loud, accusatory voice, "And You were not there for me as well when all of that was happening. And You want me to believe that You have not forgotten me?" I said to myself, *Now, I will finally find out where I will wind up.* I thought of what my mother and Robert said so often to me—it would most likely be hell.

As I continued consuming both the tablets and the whisky, I started feeling tired. I was thinking to myself, *and why do you still come back to the church after all that happened there? Why here, what was pulling me back each time?* I then finished consuming the last of the tablets and the whisky when I lost consciousness.

When I did regain consciousness and found that I was in a hospital bed. I was trying to orient myself and noticed that a man was standing to the left of the bed. I asked him who he was. He said he was a pastor and had been praying for me. I said to myself, *Oh no, not again!*

I was getting ready to ask him to leave, but he said he wanted to ask me a question. I motioned to him and, he said, "If you were able to attempt to take Your life again, would you do it?" I remembered muttering, "Yes." He continued speaking and in the middle of his sentence, I again lost consciousness.

When I awoke again, I was in a room with two beds. The first person I saw was a man sitting on the other bed. He was looking at me and showed me a slight smile and a hand wave. Then I noticed there was a doctor and a nurse standing there as well. The doctor said, "You really gave us quite a fright. After all what you went through, we thought you might not make it." I wondered what he exactly meant with that statement.

And then I looked around the room and noticed there were bars on the windows. My thoughts immediately returned to that jail cell. I began to panic and was having a hard time breathing. The doctor asked me what was wrong. I could not bring myself to tell him, and said, "I do not know where I am—is this a jail?"

He said, "No, you are not in a jail. This is a closed psychiatry ward, and you are here for Your own protection."

My own protection? In a lock up facility? Where was the protection back then, now some eleven years ago? I told him that I did not want to be here. He said that with what had happened, under the law, they would keep me here for at least three days to monitor me.

They had found out I was a soldier by the ID in my wallet. The doctor then told me that the military was notified I was here. My first thought was *absent without leave (AWOL)?* Once again, my thought was, *what punishment would I be given for this?* The doctor told me that I was in a safe place. I thought, *What safe place—in a barred-up room, with another man in it?* My mind returned to that jail cell. I should have told the doctor what had happened, but I just could not. Why did I always choose to stay silent? Just another mask, this time to hide the extreme shame and guilt.

The doctors left and I was alone with that other man, locked up together. I wondered what he had done to be here. After a period of silence, he introduced himself as Bernd. He seemed friendly enough, but still, my alert levels were on high mode.

We got to talking. I listened to him as he told his story. He went through a lot, some things similar to my experiences. It was an eye opener for me to know that someone else had gone through so much trauma and pain, along with attempted suicides and now multiple times in a psychiatry ward. I told him that I was very sorry to hear his story and that my heart went out to him. I briefly mentioned that our stories have a lot of similarities.

The door opened, and in came Michi. He came to my bed and hugged me. He said he found out from the church what happened to me and asked me how I was. He also told me that he was very worried about me. I was very glad to see him again, and I felt bad for what I had done. I told him I am sorry. He said we could talk about it later.

I introduced him to Bernd. They shook hands and exchanged brief pleasantries. I liked Bernd for some reason and I did not feel threatened by him in anyway. That was rare for me. That thought came again—*Perhaps, it will be different this time around.* How many times had I asked myself that question?

The nurse came back and told me that the doctor wanted to see me. I asked her if Michi, my good friend, could accompany me. She said that was my decision to make.

She escorted us to the doctor's office. I was wondering what was about to come.

I introduced Michi. "Oh, you are Michi?" asked the doctor. I wondered what he meant with that question. The doctor asked me how I was doing. I thought to myself, *how shall I answer that question and with which mask on?* I answered that I guess I was doing okay.

He went on to say that I should consider myself lucky to still be here among the living. I thought to myself, *Lucky? I felt just the opposite—very unlucky.*

He continued, describing to me what had happened after I was in the first psychiatric hospital. He said that, unfortunately, after I decided to not stay there, the computer had not been updated to reflect that I had left. It showed that I had been admitted and was there. And that was where he came back to Michi. He had called the hospital several times and they informed him I was there. Michi then drove to the hospital and discovered that indeed, I was not there.

And they informed the police that I was missing. They started a search with no success. The police released a missing person bulletin. A call came some thirty-six hours after I left the hospital. The church gardener had discovered me in the shed with the empty whiskey bottles and medicines, along with the suicide note and the plaque.

The doctor went on to say that being in that cold shed for that long, my body temperature had dropped to very low levels, leading to hypothermia. He said that if I had not been found as I was, I could have frozen to death.

I thought, *that would have been OK with me.*

Michi asked how such an error at the hospital could occur. Later, I would reach a substantial settlement with the hospital due to what they had conveniently covered up and called it 'a computer error".

The doctor advised me that I should stay here for a time to stabilize myself and then be transferred to the trauma station there.

What other options were available? To leave again and attempt to take my life again?

Michi visited regularly, and I had also become friends with Bernd. I had no reason to fear him. I even shared a lot of my story with him. He would listen and sketch at the same time. It turned out he was an artist. He could sketch very well and would draw pictures of how he imagined the scenes looked like as I was going through them. I told him about my bad experiences with religion and with the church. He told me that his experiences were similar.

One day, he told me that with what all I had gone through, I should consider writing a book. Where had I heard that before? I was told on several occasions that I was a good writer, and even two grammar school teachers gave me written references on how well I could write. I also still have those letter in my scrapbook. I always wondered why I had kept those items when I had destroyed so much before I decided to take my life. Maybe this was why?

I had Michi purchase me a journal book. I then started writing. In the time I was at the hospital, I filled six journals. There were written text, drawings, and so many notes. I shared some of the writing with Bernd. One day we were sitting at the table, I was writing and he started sketching. He finished sketching and then handed it to me. It was a sketch of a very narrow, rocky, and steep path, with a man trying to attempt to roll a huge stone up the mountain.

He mentioned a character called Sisyphus.

He turned out to be a mythical man who defied the gods, and in doing so, he would have to push a rock up a mountain; upon reaching the top, the rock would roll down again, leaving him to start over. He became a man who lives life to the fullest, hates death, and is condemned to a meaningless task. Later I would read about this in the boof of Ecclesiastes, referring to everything being meaningless. Meaningless in what sense, like my life, I pondered?

I asked him about the sketch and where he had got that idea. He knew that I had a Bible and asked me to open it to Matthew 7:13 and 14. I was curious. I found it and he asked me to read it aloud.

I did. "Enter by the narrow gate. For the gate is wide and the way is easy that leads to destruction, and those who enter by it are many. For the gate is narrow and the way is hard that leads to life, and those who find it are few."

Then Bernd said, "Like you, I had problems with religion, but when I saw this verse, and also read the myth about Sisyphus, it caused me to stop and really think about what this life is all about and what will happen afterwards." He started attending church after that and was going through a discipleship program. He followed that up by saying words that I heard so many times before, "Then I gave my life to Jesus, and it all changed for me."

I wondered why I always wound up being around "believers," and this time, one that has mental health issues. Before I could ask a question, he said, "You shared Your story about rejections at churches. I went through that as well, and I did not want to have anything to do with that.

Then a man entered into his life who he was able to befriend. Bernd started attending church with him and found it was a church that truly reached out to him in the midst of all of his suffering and trauma, mental health issues and all. He said that not even once did anyone there ever make him feel unwelcome or give him the feeling he was not wanted there. The man who discipled him told him one day, "I went through a lot as well. I do not exactly know Your hurt, but I know hurt and rejection. Just look and see how often Jesus was rejected." Where had I heard that before?

He went on to say that this Jesus was preaching about forgiveness of sin and repentance. And during his short thirty-three years of life, so many Jews and others rejected Him by refusing to acknowledge him as the Messiah, because Jesus was teaching contrary to what they believed and expected a Messiah would be, even with His performing so many miracles—including healing mentally sick people." In their opinion, he was a rebel and even a blasphemer worthy of death. They ultimately rejected him and crucified Him.

We looked together in the Old Testament book of Isaiah 53:3—

"He was despised and rejected by men; a man of sorrow acquainted with grief as one from who men hide their faces. He was despised, and we esteemed Him not."

That one verse changed so much inside of me. Wow, Jesus was not only despised but rejected as well? And people would not esteem him and then hide their faces from him? That sounded like a short twenty-three-word answer about my life.

Before I could say anything, Bernd said, "We both went through so much of the same things, being despised, not being loved, and complete rejection. But when I read what Jesus had endured, not to mention knowing that His own Father forsook him on the Cross, and then going back to the verses we looked in Matthew 7, those who choose to walk with Him will be required to take that very stony way and also be prepared to suffer for His namesake."

He then showed me two Corinthians 12:10. "Therefore, I am well content with weaknesses, with insults, with distresses, with persecutions, with difficulties, for Christ's sake; for when I am weak, then I am strong."

I told Bernd that this all started to make sense to me. Bernd said that if he had the ability to write a book, he would. He followed up by telling me that I had that ability, "so use that God-given gift and write, Chase, write."

And so, my primary objective—and I believe the Lord's, too—is to publish this book and help people see that they don't have to remain silent if they have gone through the same things I did. They don't have to remain silent. There is help. But I knew I could not do this for myself. But back then, times were different. One could not talk about abuse or sex—they were taboo. And who would believe me anyway? Looking back on all that happened up until then, I wish I would have had the courage to do so.

I began thinking that perhaps, Jesus had not forgotten me and would not leave me like so many others did.

Bernd told me that with what happened with us, we tend to overthink things. In the discipleship sessions, he learned that he did this because he did not grow up in a safe environment and had to take on adult duties so early in life. He said that no matter how many times he tried, he would get hurt in some way. There was so much name calling, abuse, and punishment for making mistakes.

This all led him to believe that he could never be good enough. So, he learned how to try and figure everything out on his own.

For him, this all changed when he turned to Jesus. I had heard that so many times before, but this time, it was like my eyes were being opened, and possibly my heart a bit as well?

He then finished up by telling me that he would be released from the closed ward to the trauma station in two days. I already missed him. I then had the quick thought that maybe he was one of those "angels unaware"?

My boss had also come to visit me. We met with the doctor and spoke about how things would proceed. My boss told me that I would stay in the hospital and we would figure something out. Eventually, with the serious health diagnosis (BPD and Complex PTSD), I was granted an honorable disability discharge.

Bernd was transferred to the trauma station, so I made up my mind to get myself quickly stabilized so I could go there as well. I was on yet another mission—this time with actually looking forward to what lies ahead. At that point, nothing else really mattered to me.

I wound up staying in that room alone until I got transferred. During that time, Michi would visit me. One day, he surprised me with bringing several members of the German men's national diving team, along with the coach, to visit me. They told me that they missed me at the pool and wanted me to come back as quickly. I told them that I would do that and was also looking forward to diving with them again. It was so touching!

Time went by quickly. Finally, I was deemed stabilized enough and was transferred to the trauma station.

That station had single rooms. My new room just happened to be next to Bernd's. He told me that his treatment was going very well and that he had learned so much about, in his words, "why he ticked the way he did."

The staff there were excellent, very knowledgeable and professional, and very kind. I learned so much about why "I ticked the way I did," and the therapy sessions were real eye openers. Please note that I am not a medical professional in any sense of the term. But through therapy, I learned from medical professionals the five stages of trauma. They are:

1. Denial - Your body's defense mechanism kicks in to reduce the blow of the initial and following trauma, or just outright pretending it did not happen at all.

2. Anger - This is a common response to trauma because as you at some point begin to experience or relive the memories and emotions, anger is a natural and common response. You could get angry at anything related to the trauma, or towards the people who caused the trauma. This phase can be referred to as using Your coping mechanism, the anger in you can overwhelm Your feelings, whether they be grief, pain, or sadness. In this phase, the masks come in. This phase can last a very long time, and affected people report angry outbursts when an event, inanimate objects, or a person triggers you back to the time of the trauma.

3. Bargaining - When getting over the denial and the anger phases, the very core emotions of the trauma start to become clearer. This can also be very painful in that Your feelings can be so the trauma itself and what happened become clearer. These feelings can be intense and so overwhelming that you can actually start to see what really happened and the scale of it. Here, a very common response is you wanting to control the whole situation with bargaining. Bargaining includes, but is not limited to, you wanting to have events happen differently, praying that it will go away, or even getting lost in a "what if"

this had not happened or that something else did instead of Your trauma.

It is important to note here, especially as is relates to me, that I leaned very heavily on religion, praying constantly to have the trauma taken away, for example, asking God to heal. As you have read up until this point, you can clearly see my heavy leaning on religion. But it should not be a religion that I had been searching for—perhaps it was a relationship - with Jesus?.

4. Depression - After bargaining has run its course, The next phase that occurs is depression. Being angry and bargaining can be very "alive," whereas depression takes you into a more quiet and slower stage. Here starts the overwhelming weight of what really happened, which is, a lot of the time, too much to bear. This is when sadness, emptiness, hopelessness, trouble sleeping, lethargy, and a loss of interest in what you once found very enjoyable. In my case, it was the springboard diving. Then the guilt, blame, and shame start, along with either reduced or increased eating. In my case, I almost stopped eating altogether. Withdrawal was very big for me. I just wanted to be on my own and not see anyone. It's like the lyrics of the Simon and Garfunkel song, "Hello darkness, my old friend……"

During this stage, therapy might begin, along with prescribed medicines such as selective serotonin reuptake inhibitors (SSRIs); serotonin and noradrenaline reuptake inhibitors (SNRIs); tricyclic antidepressants (TCAs), such as amitriptyline or imipramine, and others.

5. Acceptance - This last phase of trauma helps you move forward toward healing, or acceptance. Here you have processed and acknowledged what happened to you and you find Yourself in a much better place when it comes to dealing with the consequences of the traumatic event. Acceptance can seem to entail forgiving those who hurt you, and in doing so, accepting that the trauma actually happened to you. What occurs in this last phase is that you have accepted the trauma experiences and also how the trauma has changed Your life. It means you've come to terms with Your experience and how it has changed Your life.

In this stage, it is very important to ask for help from friends or mental health professionals. I learned at some point that you have every right to be proud of all the work you have accomplished to have reached this stage of acceptance.

I sat down and wrote all five stages out and recorded that I went through each of these stages. It was excruciating.

The time there just flew by. One therapist whom I worked with had to remind me many times that what happened to me in my early childhood was not my fault. She said that we would work on tapping into my "inner child." I had no idea what that was.

As I learned, the wounds I sustained as a young boy from the result of trauma, abuse, and abandonment (especially from my parents and foster parents), were most likely the main source of my experiencing emotional needs that were never met, and being raised in a very broken family environment. And then there was the severe sexual abuse that needed to be addressed. It was overwhelming, but my therapist spent a great deal of time with me. The group sessions were helpful to me as it was the first time that I was not alone in this, and that others also had also been exposed to so much trauma. The group sessions were very therapeutic for me.

On one Sunday, a pastor held a service at the clinic. His sermon was titled "Jesus and 11th Hour Christians." I thought it was an odd title. Basically, the sermon was about his forty years of preaching the gospel to "the lost." He went on to speak about Jesus' forgiveness and offer of salvation being available until our dying breath. And then he stated that he would find it greatly unfair, having faithfully served the Lord for so long, to die and discover that "an 11th hour Christian" (those who accepted Christ as Savior in the last hours or so of their lives) was standing in the line in front of him to get into Heaven.

He said that angered him. Well, it angered me, as well, as I could not believe that he would first preach on the offer of forgiveness and salvation until death and then turn with 180 degrees on "those Christians"? Even I knew that what he was saying was absolutely untrue. As he spoke, it just angered me more. I made up my mind right then that I would confront him after the service and "give him a piece of my mind."

After the service concluded, I waited until the others were all gone and then followed him to his office.

I said to him that I had to speak to him because I found his sermon very offensive and selfish on his part. I asked him who he thought he was with preaching such heresy. I told him that I while I was listening to his "garbage" (I was truly enraged by this sermon), I felt it was my duty to show him just what I meant. I remember learning about the laborers in the vineyard story in Matthew 20:1–16. I began reading it to him, the intonation with each word growing sharper with emphasis.

"For the kingdom of heaven is like a master of a house who went out early in the morning to hire laborers for his vineyard. After agreeing with the laborers for a denarius a day, he sent them into his vineyard. And going out about the third hour he saw others standing idle in the marketplace, and to them he said, 'You go into the vineyard too, and whatever is right I will give you.' So they went. Going out again about the sixth hour and the ninth hour, he did the same. And about the eleventh hour he went out and found others standing. And he said to them, 'Why do you stand here idle all day?' They said to him, 'Because no one has hired us.' He said to them, 'You go into the vineyard too.' And when evening came, the owner of the vineyard said to his foreman, 'Call the laborers and pay them their wages, beginning with the last, up to the first.' And when those hired about the eleventh hour came, each of them received a denarius. Now when those hired first came, they thought they would receive more, but each of them also received a denarius. And on receiving it they grumbled at the master of the house, saying, 'These last worked only one hour, and you have made them equal to us who have borne the burden of the day and the scorching heat.' But he replied to one of them, 'Friend, I am doing you no wrong. Did you not agree with me for a denarius? Take what belongs to you and go. I choose to give to this last worker as I give to you. Am I not allowed to do what I choose with what belongs to me? Or do you begrudge my generosity?' **So the last will be first, and the first last."**

"So, I am certain with that story that Jesus did not think that way. So, what do you think about that?" He was stunned and appeared to be speechless. I thought to myself, *Chase, you finally did it. You spoke Your mind with conviction, and you really showed him a thing or two.* I was proud of myself. I did it. You zapped him. I had those thoughts so many times and just could not go through with converting them into words.

There was silence. Did I find myself actually defending the Word of God?" I thought, *where did that come from?*

I did not even want to hear an answer from him and my desire was to just get up and storm out of the room.

As we both stood up, the pastor said, "You are correct in what you stated. I was wrong for preaching that."

And then the strangest thing happened. As we both stood up, the pastor came to me and hugged me, saying, "Even us old geezers need this kind of reminders.

He asked me and then God to forgive him. He went on to say, "God bless you for what you did, standing on conviction and truth."

I was stunned. Me standing on conviction and truth? I thought for sure that he would have shot back, rejected me, and tell me to leave. But he did not. He simply admitted to me that he was wrong and asked for forgiveness.

We stood there together, looking at each other, both of us deep in our own thoughts.

In that moment, I felt the oddest feeling come over me. I felt such warmth and love, and at the same time that great conviction and truth that he was speaking about.

I found myself falling to my knees and pleading with the Lord, "I cannot do this any longer, I have no fight left in me. I do believe that You are the Son of God and came to live as a man and be crucified to atone for my very wicked and abominable sins. I confess all of this to You and humbly ask You for Your forgiveness. I call on You to come into my heart, Lord.

As I opened my eyes, the pastor was kneeled beside me and was praising God for his greatness, power, and glory. A lost sheep had finally been found. This, dear reader, is the power of the Holy Spirit at work.

I could not believe what just happened. The pain, abuse, rejection, marginalization, abandonment, deception, immorality, lying, and most importantly my pride—I had just surrendered them all. My life was made new. I knew in that moment that the past was gone and it had no power over me. I had been redeemed, purchased by the precious blood of Jesus Christ.

For the first time in my life, I felt free. No need to wear a mask, and certainly not a hollow one any longer. I was a new person in Christ Jesus, and realizing this for the first time in my life, I knew where my ultimate destiny in eternity would be—with Him, my Lord and Savior, to whom all honor and glory are ascribed. It was a great step to begin removing those hollow masks, and He helped me do this, step by step—that's called sanctification. I love this Bible verse in John 8:36 - "So, if the Son sets you free, you will be free indeed."

And that I was! No longer a slave to sin! And I learned that when Satan comes and reminds me of my past, I turn to him and remind him of his future!

I thought about the chief and that verse in Isaiah 49:16: See, I will not forget you for I have carved Your name on the palms of MY hands (Isaiah 49:16). That plaque is prominently displayed in the apartment.

Christ Jesus truly did not forget me, and he literally stayed with me through all the horrors of my life until He made me one of His own. I finished up with the therapy. One of the biggest achievements was letting Hannah go. I never saw or heard from her again.

An even greater achievement was learning about what true forgiveness is. So to my parents, my foster parents, Chuck, Teri, Lisa, and all of those who abused and betrayed me, I forgive you completely from my heart! Forgiveness brought freedom! And yes, Robert, I made it. I became a man, a man in my own right!

I was allowed to stay in Germany and become a permanent resident. Michi allowed me to move in with him. I attended his church and was baptized there. I asked his pastor if another pastor could baptize me. He said yes. The baptism was conducted by the pastor who gave that 11th Hour sermon and wound-up kneeling with me as I accepted Christ as my Savior.

My baptism was truly a very special moment when I publicly acknowledged my old self was buried with Christ and I had been raised to new life in Jesus! Just before being completely immersed in the water, the pastor said, "Chase, I now baptize you in the name of the Father, the Son, and of the Holy Spirit!"

And the wonderful and special highlight of that moment is where I was baptized. You guessed it - in the Munich diving pool! Surrounded by diving buddies, friends and brothers and sisters in Jesus, several who, after hearing my story, also went on to surrender their lives to Christ!

I continued growing in Christ, discovering my gifts of evangelism, hospitality and encouragement. I also continued with diving and other sports. I enrolled in university and obtained my degree in psychology, majoring in trauma and behavioral therapy. My desire was to help others who went through what I did, hopefully identifying the trauma much earlier in life. And that is what God allowed me to do. This verse means so much to me. I personalized it just for me!

Ephesians 2:10 - "For I, Chase, am His workmanship, created in Christ Jesus for good works, which God prepared beforehand, that I should walk in them."

I think back to all of those verses in the beginning of this story speaking about who we are in Christ. They did not make a lot of sense way back then, but now they have become a huge part of my life.

All these are the answer to my question, posed here in this book several times—who am I? First, I am born again (my memories returned to Reverend Moore; this time very positive thoughts, and actually looking forward to meeting him one day in eternity).

But for me, the real question is not "who am I?" but rather "whose am I?" The resounding answer to that question is Him, the Lord Jesus Christ, and glory be to Him!

Another truly special friend, recently sent this note to me after completing this manuscript. "Chase, that's good news! A big step has been taken and I hope you are happy that you completed the manuscript. What a hard road, walked with courage, a lot of strength, and at times great exhaustion. I know that it is a relief for you. I know with all my heart that this has brought healing and inner peace for you! I can only say again and again that I have the greatest respect and congratulate you from the bottom of my heart. I am proud of you! Kind regards, Karin".

"Proud of you?" Here they finally were, confirmation. Those are the words that I had longed to hear on so many occasions. That touched my heart in a very special way! Thank you, Karin!

One of my favorite verses is Isaiah 41:10 - "I have chosen you and not cast you off; fear not, for I am with you; be not dismayed, for I am Your God. I will strengthen you; I will help you; I will uphold you with my righteous right hand."

Under new management!

He works in strange ways!

Milton Keynes UK
Ingram Content Group UK Ltd.
UKHW020733131123
432470UK00020B/1030